Capital (R)evolution

Patricio M. Danziger with Maximiliano Figueroa

Capital (R)evolution

Nine Global Phenomena Impacting Your Investment Portfolio

palgrave
macmillan

Patricio M. Danziger
Eternal Capital Group, Miami, FL, USA

Collaborator
Maximiliano Figueroa
Ciudad Autónoma de Buenos Aires,
Buenos Aires, Argentina

ISBN 978-3-032-31601-1 ISBN 978-3-032-31602-8 (eBook)
https://doi.org/10.1007/978-3-032-31602-8

Cover Credit: SWKStock/shutterstock

This Palgrave Macmillan imprint is published by the registered company Springer Nature Switzerland AG
The registered company address is: Gewerbestrasse 11, 6330 Cham, Switzerland

Preface

I grew up in a house filled with books, and that early fascination with knowledge has never left me. Sharing ideas has always been my way of understanding the world. My desire was to put in writing what I have learned over more than twenty years of my fortunate and fascinating career. Over the years, I have interviewed presidents, ministers, industry experts, analysts, journalists, CEOs, and management teams of more than a thousand companies in every industry around the world. I have invested in over one hundred companies. Every meeting, every journey, and every conversation has contributed to the reflections that now converge in these pages.

Secondly, my desire is to connect thought with action. Capital (R)evolution is not just a book—it reflects the intellectual foundations that also inspire the work of Eternal Capital Group. It embodies a disciplined way of thinking—grounded in analysis and independent judgment. The relationship between writing and investing is circular—markets test ideas, and ideas give meaning to practice.

If this book helps readers see the world's transformations with more clarity or inspires them to invest with greater purpose, then it will have fulfilled its mission.

Miami, United States　　　　Patricio M. Danziger

Competing Interest Patricio M. Danziger is the founder and CIO of Eternal Capital Group. The company did not finance, commission, or otherwise influence the research or writing of this book.

Maximiliano Figueroa is an independent consultant for Eternal Capital Group and collaborated in every aspect of the book.

The authors declare no conflicts of interest relevant to the content of this book.

About the Book

Who has not dreamed of traveling through time to change decisions and behaviors that did not turn out as expected? This book is not exactly a journey to modify the past but a guide to understand the future. It offers a look at nine global phenomena that will define our world over the next twenty years—captured just before they become everyday reality. P.M. Danziger gathers enlightening research, interviews with world leaders, and investment cases that explore some of the most pressing fears and opportunities of the future—forces that will soon impact our daily lives and shape the most relevant investment themes of the next two decades.

From the still-unimagined uses of artificial intelligence and the automation of everyday processes to the mass adoption of electric vehicles and the consolidation of autonomous driving—changes almost as profound as the transition from horse-drawn carriages to automobiles. From how blockchain and cryptocurrency technologies will redefine how we save and revolutionize the industries on which our existence depends to the most transformative ways of producing energy. From the medicine of the future, which will offer treatments for diseases once considered incurable, to the new patterns of mass consumption that are reshaping global demand.

Capital (R)evolution is a guide to understanding the world that lies ahead—before the future is written. Its in-depth analysis of emerging phenomena helps investors, advisors, and consultants better understand market shifts, identify high-potential opportunities, and offer more informed guidance in a rapidly changing world.

About the Author

Patricio M. Danziger is an economist and MBA graduate of the Booth School of Business at the University of Chicago. He is the Founder and CIO of Eternal Capital Group, a global investment firm focused on emerging markets. With more than twenty years of experience as an institutional investor, he has received several international distinctions, including recognition for managing the world's best-performing fund in its category in 2021. Previously, he was a partner and member of the Investment Committee for Emerging Market Strategies at Redwheel—one of the top-performing global funds in that category between 2015 and 2022—and head of Global Thematic Research at Redwheel's Emerging Markets team. Earlier in his career, he served as managing director and portfolio manager at Everest Capital. Guided by his passions for writing, research, and investing, Patricio brings to life nine transformative themes that he believes will continue to redefine the future of emerging markets. In this book, he blends insight and experience to reveal how both top-down and bottom-up perspectives shape his investment philosophy and how these forces are driving some of the most compelling opportunities around the world. His personality and values were shaped by competing as a tennis player since he was young. Patricio plays the guitar and is passionate about music.

About the Collaborator

Maximiliano Figueroa holds an MBA from the University of Virginia Darden School of Business and has nearly two decades of experience across consulting, investment banking, and asset management. His work focuses on thematic research and strategic communication, examining how long-term structural forces such as technological change, demographic shifts, and capital flows translate into investment frameworks, sector dynamics, and equity market opportunities, particularly in emerging markets. He works closely with an emerging markets equity fund, contributing to thematic research, investment process development, investor communications, and strategic positioning. Outside finance, he is an opera singer and a speaker on cultural and philosophical topics.

Acknowledgements

First and foremost, I would like to thank my wife, Maria Paz Casinelli. She not only always encourages me to pursue my dreams and is my first enthusiast but also is the rock and foundation of our family. But if that were not enough, she helped me initially with some of the research that I included in the book. To my kids, who give me pure love and unimaginable strength and make me want to be a better person every day. My deepest gratitude goes to my parents, who nurtured my curiosity and filled our home with books—an environment that shaped everything I have done since. To my brother and his family as well, whom I love and respect.

I am especially grateful to Maximiliano Figueroa, my collaborator throughout every stage of this project. His insight, dedication, and intellectual companionship have been invaluable. I thank Florencia Grieco for her valuable assistance in refining the language and style of the manuscript. I also wish to thank my partners at Eternal Capital Group, whose trust and shared vision continue to inspire the work we do.

My sincere appreciation goes to John Willig, my literary agent, for his guidance and professionalism; and to the editorial team at Palgrave Macmillan, for believing in this project and helping bring it to life.

Last but not least, I would like to thank the people that collaborated on the book in some way: Federico Kattan, Federico Sturzenegger, Lucas Grosman, Frederik Mishkin, Mariano Federici, Carlos Roberts, and Guilherme Ximenes Almeida.

Contents

Part I

A New World

1

The Reinvention of the Wheel: Autonomous and Electric Vehicles

We're going to invent tomorrow instead of worrying about what happened yesterday.
Steve Jobs

Throughout human history, few developments have sparked more hopeful visions of the future than transportation. From the invention of the wheel more than three millennia before Christ to the flying *Back to the Future* DeLorean; from Carl Benz's first patented automobile in 1886 and the Wright brothers' flying machine in 1903 to humankind's arrival on the Moon and dreams of reaching Mars; from Leonardo da Vinci's visionary sketches to Elon Musk's disruptive imagination—human creations linked to transport have consistently shattered old paradigms and generated new fantasies, revolutionizing how we live in the present while paving the way toward an entirely different idea of the future.

Today, once again, the transportation industry—one of the world's largest—is undergoing a transformation comparable only to the late-19th-century shift from the horse-drawn carriage to the internal-combustion automobile. It is a revolution poised to change the world as we know it. We are not (yet) making teleportation real or achieving time travel, but the changes we'll witness in how we move across the planet could easily rival those dreams.

Soon, we may no longer drive our own cars: our cars will drive themselves. Owing to the rapid evolution of artificial intelligence, autonomous vehicles will become reality much sooner than most imagine—practically around the corner. And the implications for daily life are immense: far fewer accidents, greater efficiency in urban traffic through shared mobility, and the

P. M. Danziger, *Capital (R)evolution*,
https://doi.org/10.1007/978-3-032-31602-8_1

acceleration of clean-energy adoption as the internal-combustion engine fades away, among many other social and personal benefits.

Without adopting a naively optimistic view that ignores the complex ways AI and robotics could reshape labor markets, the time has come to stop asking *when* self-driving technology will arrive and to start thinking—right now—about what will come after.

From Leonardo da Vinci to Elon Musk and Wang Chuanfu

Surprisingly, the concept of autonomous vehicles dates back to 1495. The quintessential Renaissance inventor, Leonardo da Vinci, designed a self-propelled cart controlled by gears and pulleys—considered the ancestor of the modern automobile. Fast-forward to 1925, when American electrical engineer Francis Houdina built a radio-controlled car; then to 1939, when industrial designer Norman Bel Geddes presented a driverless vehicle at the New York World's Fair. Human ingenuity has always aimed at transportation, and in the modern era it's difficult to imagine inventions more intertwined with ideas of progress and prosperity than trains, airplanes, and cars. Transport carried us to the present—and it will carry us into the future.

Yet it wasn't until the 1980s that autonomous vehicles gained real traction. In 1980, German engineer Ernst Dickmanns developed a self-driving car capable of reaching 100 km/h on empty roads. By 1987, his car could navigate public highways, and by 1995 it was running on the autobahn. A few years later, in 1999, the system could already recognize traffic signs. In the 2000s, autonomous vehicles caught the attention of tech giants. In 2009—when innovation and Google were practically synonymous—the company began developing its own prototypes; Uber joined the race in 2015. Through the 2010s the technology matured, venturing into real-world environments. Research on unmanned systems by the U.S. Defense Advanced Research Projects Agency (DARPA) gave another crucial boost, and in 2010 Google launched its autonomous-vehicle pilot program in California.

But when we talk about self-driving cars, one name is unavoidable: Elon Musk. Tesla has been testing autonomous vehicles since 2015, accumulating over 10 billion miles of self-driving data and becoming one of the global leaders in the field. Musk's achievements are even greater: he and Tesla have ensured that even those with little technological knowledge are aware that self-driving vehicles already exist.

Tesla's autonomous vehicles rely on multiple sensors enabling them to perceive and interpret their surroundings. The system uses machine-learning algorithms to decide how to drive. Tesla's *Full Self-Driving Supervised*—an advanced driver-assistance system still requiring constant human oversight—has shown it can handle varied traffic conditions. Just as Carl Benz patented the world's first three-wheeled "gasoline-powered vehicle," capable of a top speed of 16 km/h, on January 29, 1886, Tesla now plans to launch robotaxis in several U.S. cities. Success, as history reminds us, depends not merely on invention but on turning a brilliant idea into a mass product capable of altering social and economic life.

While Tesla was founded in 2003 by Martin Eberhard and Marc Tarpenning and named in honor of Serbian-American inventor Nikola Tesla, Elon Musk joined as chairman in 2004 and became CEO in 2008. Musk is credited worldwide with transforming Tesla into the giant it is today: a leader in electric vehicles, clean energy, and autonomous-driving technology.

Tesla has continued refining its long-awaited Version 12 of *Full Self-Driving* (FSD), now branded *FSD Supervised*, based on end-to-end AI. Although it has made major progress, it still requires human intervention in some cases.[1]

Earlier iterations fell short of expectations—so much so that, in 2021, Musk himself admitted with his trademark bluntness that version 9.2 "wasn't great." In January 2024, industry outlets highlighted posts on X by Ashok Elluswamy (@aelluswamy), the program's director, showing an FSD V12-driven car deftly avoiding a large puddle and another executing a perfect U-turn.

While Tesla's journey has included incidents—such as a fatal accident in 2016—autonomous-driving tests have been comparatively safe, managing the inherent risks of early-stage scientific exploration. As any rational company would, Tesla has strengthened its safety systems, adding protective features and increasing human supervision.

There is no invention without risk; creation is impossible without error. The goal is not to be born perfect but to see beyond the limits of the moment and improve as quickly as possible—the hallmark of every great visionary. That holds especially true for Musk and Tesla, the most visible players on the autonomous-vehicle map, though far from the only ones.

Larry Page, Google's co-founder alongside Sergey Brin, recently reflected on how the revolution that Google sparked three decades ago continues in today's race toward autonomy: "We founded Google because we're very optimistic

---

[1] Autopilot Review, "Full Self-Driving Update," https://www.autopilotreview.com/full-self-driving-update (Accessed October 26, 2025)

about technology's potential to make the world a better place. Think of how many people lack adequate transportation—like those with disabilities—and how self-driving cars will transform their lives. Or the time you waste every day commuting. Or the deaths and injuries that could be avoided."

By July 2015, Google's early driverless cars had logged over 1 million miles with only fourteen minor incidents—and in every case, the autonomous vehicle was not at fault. Uber launched its own pilot program in Pittsburgh a year later, partnering with Volvo and announcing a "third-generation" vehicle designed to operate without a driver. In 2020 it sold its self-driving unit to Aurora Innovation[2]—a startup founded by former Google and Tesla engineers, led by Chris Urmson, the former head of Google's self-driving project before it became Waymo. The same tech ecosystem that reshaped the world a few decades ago is doing so once more. Waymo already operates fully driverless robotaxi fleets in multiple U.S. cities, completing hundreds of thousands of paid rides each week and demonstrating that Level 4 autonomy can scale as a software platform rather than a labor model.

Indeed, the scope and promise of the autonomous-vehicle market can be gauged by the sheer number of household names involved: Tesla and Google. Apple launched its autonomous *Project Titan* in 2015 and shut it down in 2024. And Wang Chuanfu, the visionary Chinese engineer-entrepreneur who founded Build Your Dreams (BYD), began his career in the 1990s making rechargeable batteries and, through long-term vision, turned his company into one of the world's largest electric-vehicle manufacturers. BYD's vertical integration—from battery production to the manufacture of electric cars and buses—allowed it to cut costs and dominate China's domestic market while expanding into Europe and Latin America. Under Wang's leadership, the company surpassed Tesla in global EV sales across several recent quarters; in China, it holds about 32% market share versus 6.1% for Tesla (2024).[3] BYD also built its first factory in Brazil, investing roughly $600 million. And if one more player was missing, it was Amazon. In 2020, the company acquired Zoox—an autonomous vehicle startup founded in 2014—created to deliver mobility "not as a better car, but as an entirely new form of transport, designed to be driven by AI and enjoyed by humans."

For us to *enjoy* self-driving cars, however, one major step remains: regulators and the public must trust them. But before long, the right question

[2] Andrew J. Hawkins, "Uber's fraught and deadly pursuit of self-driving cars is over," *The Verge*, December 7, 2020, https://www.theverge.com/2020/12/7/22158745/uber-selling-autonomous-vehicle-business-aurora-innovation (Accessed October 26, 2025).

[3] *CNN*, "China's BYD annual sales pass Tesla," March 25, 2025, https://edition.cnn.com/2025/03/25/cars/china-byd-annual-sales-pass-tesla-intl-hnk (Accessed October 26, 2025).

should change to: Why is it even legal for humans to drive? According to the World Health Organization, traffic accidents are the eighth leading cause of death worldwide.

The Future Arrives

Naturally, all these private-sector initiatives are beginning to find an echo in public policy. By 2018, twenty-nine U.S. states already allowed the testing of autonomous vehicles on their roads. These programs were aimed both at validating self-driving technology and at studying the public's attitude and behavior toward it. In Las Vegas and Phoenix, self-driving cars are being tested alongside regular drivers, while the state of California has approved their sale, and the autonomous-vehicle company Cruise[4] launched a robotaxi service in San Francisco before GM ended the program in December 2024—just a few of the pioneering cases. Like it or not, autonomous vehicles are already on the road, narrowing the gap that separates them from what we still call "normal" cars and edging closer to the moment when they will drastically and permanently reshape the transport and logistics industries—and, as a result, our daily lives.

With respect to the artificial intelligence component of autonomous vehicles, one of the greatest challenges is advancing through the levels of automation. AVs operate on a three-phase design known as "sense–plan–act," the same basic logic behind many robotic systems (and, arguably, a fair description of our own most rational behavior). To understand complex and dynamic driving environments such as modern cities, autonomous vehicles are equipped with sensors, cameras, and radars that collect environmental data. That information is processed by software that determines the next actions—accelerating, braking, or changing lanes. Typically, a combination of radar, cameras, and LiDAR (Light Detection and Ranging) is used. LiDAR is a remote-sensing technology that employs laser pulses to measure distance and create 3D maps of objects and surroundings.[5] Google relies on LiDAR sensors, while Tesla primarily uses cameras. LiDAR sensors that once cost tens of thousands of dollars per vehicle have fallen to below $1,000 in some automotive-grade configurations, accelerating commercial adoption.

[4] Kirsten Korosec, "Cruise can now test driverless vehicles on the streets of San Francisco," *TechCrunch*, October 15, 2020, https://techcrunch.com/2020/10/15/cruise-can-now-test-driverless-vehicles-on-the-streets-of-san-francisco (Accessed October 26, 2025).

[5] *SpringerLink*, "Autonomous Vehicles: Challenges, Opportunities, and Future Implications for Transportation Policies," August 29, 2016, https://link.springer.com/chapter/10.1007/978-3-319-40503-2_5 (Accessed October 26, 2025).

High-resolution mapping for autonomous driving generates extremely large data volumes, turning detailed road geometry and environmental mapping into a valuable strategic data asset.

By 2026, over-the-air software updates allow automakers to improve battery management, efficiency, and power delivery, sometimes increasing usable range or sharpening acceleration without physical modifications. While improvements vary by model, software has become a meaningful performance lever alongside hardware.

Automation levels, which depend on how much control the vehicle retains versus the driver, range from 0 (no automation) to 5 (full automation). At Levels 1 and 2 the human still monitors the trip. Some automakers have achieved Level 2+ systems—hands-free driving, though the driver must remain alert. Level 3 lets the system drive autonomously except when it requests human intervention. Levels 4 and 5 require none at all; the car monitors its own environment and performs all safety-critical functions.

Dieter Zetsche, who led Mercedes-Benz for thirteen years, described autonomous cars memorably: "We are witnessing the fusion of several worlds—the tech industry, the Internet, and the automotive industry. This fusion is like a smartphone on wheels—or, put differently, a car endowed with many of the capabilities of smartphones and computers." Unlike computers or phones, however, not all autonomous vehicles are electric. They can be powered by gasoline, diesel, hybrids, hydrogen fuel cells, or batteries. Propulsion is independent of autonomy—but public perception links the two, largely thanks to Tesla, where indeed all autonomous cars are electric.

There is another crucial distinction: autonomous cars will have a far greater impact on the auto industry than electric ones. With EVs, the major change lies in the powertrain, which accounts for roughly 20–30 percent of added value. Autonomous vehicles, by contrast, transform value creation across every aspect of development—from design to assembly, from software to data management.

Compared with a standard car, the workforce required to produce an autonomous one varies with the technology, the plant's level of automation, and design complexity. Many steps in conventional car making—assembly, welding, painting—are already automated, but substantial manual labor remains. Autonomous vehicles demand more sophisticated technology and thus greater manufacturing complexity, relying on technicians specialized in electronics, sensors, and software. Electric cars, meanwhile, may need fewer operators because their motors are simpler—but more because their batteries are not. In the 1970s, electronics were a tiny 5% of a car's cost, mostly simple microchips used for the first electronic fuel injections. Today, as cars transform into "computers on wheels," electronics and software account for 40% of the cost and are projected to exceed 50% in fully autonomous models.

Today's major concern is technological substitution—a new technology that replaces or redefines business practices and, in doing so, reshapes labor markets. Just as e-commerce disrupted consumer habits and forced a painful restructuring of brick-and-mortar retail, autonomous vehicles—especially trucks—will replace much of the professional driving workforce.

And at the core of this change lies a transformative concept: robotaxis. Companies such as Waymo already operate commercial robotaxi services; Tesla is developing its own full self-driving system with future robotaxi capabilities. Amazon's Zoox focuses on autonomous vehicles for mobility and delivery; GM's Cruise tested driverless fleets in urban settings until the program was shut down; Aptiv develops both self-driving technology and mobility solutions. All are at the frontier of autonomous mobility, aiming to redefine urban transportation.

House Rules

Each autonomous vehicle could replace up to ten conventional ones—especially if used in shared-transport mode—meaning a smaller autonomous fleet could serve the same population. If AVs can double highway capacity by eliminating the variability of human drivers, it is equally true that labor makes up about 40 percent of trucking costs, so adopters will realize savings immediately. In the United States, operating a haul truck costs an average of $2.34 per mile. Drivers are increasingly hard to find. The U.S. freight industry currently faces a shortage of about 80,000 drivers—a consequence of grueling hours and multi-day trips. Truckers are prohibited from driving more than 11 hours per day without an eight-hour rest, yet a driverless truck could run 24 hours nonstop.

Trucking is also dangerous. Large trucks were involved in more than 5,700 fatalities in 2022, a number that has risen steadily for a decade despite falling passenger-vehicle deaths. Truck driving is now considered the most hazardous job in America. The solution is clear but complex: make some trucks drive themselves, using AI to cover the labor shortfall and improve safety.[6]

Safety remains the central concern. Autonomous trucks will reduce road deaths by eliminating human error—the cause of most crashes—but they

[6] *Amazon Web Services (AWS)*, "TuSimple Uses AI to Train Self-Driving Semis," https://aws.amazon.com/machine-learning/customers/innovators/tusimple/ (Accessed October 26, 2025).

bring new risks. Chief among them are system failures and cybersecurity threats. These systems are enormously complex, requiring vast datasets for training. Even the best can err, with potentially fatal consequences. Because AVs collect and process huge amounts of data, they are also targets for hackers who could disable or even seize control of a vehicle. To address these risks, manufacturers employ redundancy—multiple systems performing the same task so that if one fails, others compensate—and advanced error-detection and prevention software.

Autonomous-vehicle laws can be national or local. States and provinces determine where AVs may operate and who is liable in case of accidents. In the U.S., for example, California requires manufacturers to obtain permits for public-road testing and has set detailed operating rules. Arizona, by contrast, has adopted a more permissive stance, allowing broader testing with fewer restrictions.

Some countries impose strict liability, meaning the manufacturer or owner is responsible for damages. Others—like the U.S. and Germany—apply mixed systems.

In Florida, a federal jury ordered Tesla to pay $243 million for partial responsibility in a 2019 fatal Autopilot crash, citing Elon Musk's claim that Autopilot "drives better than a human.[7]" In Germany, liability arises only in cases of fault or negligence. In Shenzhen, China, municipal regulations apply; in Germany, enforcement falls to the Federal Motor Transport Authority. Both designate specific areas for AV operation—high-traffic highways with speed limits, for instance. In Shenzhen the vehicle owner bears liability; in Germany, Mercedes-Benz has publicly committed to assuming responsibility for Level 3 accidents whenever autonomous mode is engaged. A major regulatory milestone is UN-R157, which establishes global standards for approving advanced driver-assistance systems (automated lane keeping systems, or ALKS) and autonomous vehicles. According to the rule: an ALKS is a driver-activated system that keeps the vehicle within its lane at speeds up to 60 km/h by controlling lateral and longitudinal movements for extended periods without driver intervention.

Issued by the United Nations Economic Commission for Europe (UNECE), UN-R157 promotes both safety and interoperability on international roads. It defines technical and performance requirements to ensure that autonomous systems are reliable, and it mandates the recording and exchange

[7] *Reuters*, "Tesla Ordered by Florida Jury to Pay $243 Million for Fatal Autopilot Crash," August 1, 2025, https://www.reuters.com/legal/litigation/tesla-ordered-by-florida-jury-pay-243-million-fatal-autopilot-crash-2025-08-01/ (Accessed October 26, 2025).

of operational data for supervision. While not yet legally binding everywhere, it is rapidly gaining traction as a global benchmark.

Beyond safety, automation will inevitably cut jobs for car, bus, and truck drivers. If Uber were to launch its own self-driving fleet—or if its users switched to Waymo—more than 8 million drivers worldwide could lose their livelihoods. (The U.S. alone has about 3.5 million truck drivers and roughly 50 million professional drivers worldwide.[8]) Tesla illustrates the structural shift: a hyper-efficient company with fewer workers. Unlike traditional automakers that rely on dealership networks, Tesla sells mostly online—requiring far less staff. I own a Tesla myself: I bought it online like an iPhone, and it was delivered to my door—no middleman involved.

American labor unions[9] have already raised the alarm. Sean M. O'Brien, president of the International Brotherhood of Teamsters, said: "Hundreds of thousands of people make their living turning a key, so we are firmly committed to working with Congress and federal regulators to get autonomous-vehicle policy right.[10]" As always, innovation triggers tension, and this time it speeds along the regulatory lane: the Teamsters are pressing lawmakers to ensure that automation doesn't erode workers' rights.

A case in point is TuSimple, a Chinese autonomous-trucking company that set out to revolutionize freight by eliminating drivers and cutting operating costs by 50 percent (40 percent from removing the driver and 10 percent from fuel efficiency). TuSimple already runs autonomous fleets in China, but its U.S. plans stumbled despite a major headquarters in San Diego. In early 2024 the company announced its withdrawal from Nasdaq as part of a strategy to exit the American market.

The autonomous-vehicle market was valued at $55 billion in 2022 and could reach $400 billion by 2035, a compound annual growth rate of 17 percent.[11] That surge will drastically reshape the insurance industry. As early as 2017, insurers were preparing for a long-term decline in auto premiums as safer AVs spread, while exploring new opportunities. Accenture projected that three new business lines—cybersecurity, product-liability coverage for

[8] American Trucking Associations (ATA), "Truck Driver Shortage Analysis," https://www.trucking.org/ (Accessed October 26, 2025).

[9] *Bloomberg Law*, "Teamsters, Tech Firms Tangle Over Self-Driving Trucks Bill," March 13, 2023, https://news.bloomberglaw.com/daily-labor-report/teamsters-tech-firms-tangle-over-self-driving-trucks-bill (Accessed October 26, 2025).

[10] *International Brotherhood of Teamsters*, "Teamsters Release AV Policy Framework," September 12, 2023, https://teamster.org/2023/09/teamsters-release-av-policy-framework/ (Accessed October 26, 2025).

[11] *McKinsey & Company*, "Autonomous Driving's Future: Convenient and Connected," January 6, 2023 https://www.mckinsey.com/industries/automotive-and-assembly/our-insights/autonomous-drivings-future-convenient-and-connected (Accessed October 26, 2025).

defective sensors or algorithms, and public-infrastructure insurance—could generate billions of dollars in new U.S. auto-insurance premiums. Forward-looking firms were already positioning themselves to seize the first-mover advantage.

In essence, the challenge mirrors that of the labor market: finding new revenue streams as old models expire. Most analysts agree that autonomous cars will be substantially safer than human-driven ones, cutting traffic deaths and insurance costs. Taxi, bus, and ride-hail drivers will become unnecessary; productivity will surge, and transportation costs will fall.

As with many AI-driven industries, labor is the flashpoint. But this is not simple arithmetic—nothing about the future ever is. It represents a profound transformation of the sector and, with it, of the labor market. As Elon Musk likes to say: "When Henry Ford made cheap, reliable cars, people said, 'What's wrong with a horse?' That was a big bet—and it worked."

Electric Dreams

Just as autonomous vehicles will soon redefine the automotive industry, electric vehicles will become the main drivers of the planet's decarbonization. We stand at the dawn of a revolution whose full scope is hard to measure today—but within a few short years it will have transformed far more than the way we travel. It will have changed, above all, the way we relate to one another and to the planet itself.

If the world's 1.4 billion vehicles were electric with average battery sizes around 60 kWh, they could collectively store roughly 80 to 90 TWh of energy. Through Vehicle-to-Grid technology, EVs could function not just as consumers, but as flexible energy assets that support grid stability during peak demand.

Since Nikola Tesla—the genius who dreamed of electrifying everything—we have known that electricity is, on average, a cleaner energy source than oil. But that is not enough: electricity generation grows cleaner every year as renewables expand. Unsurprisingly, electric-vehicle sales have soared in the past three years and will continue rising throughout the next decade.

Incredibly, the story of electric cars goes back more than two centuries. In 1832, Scottish businessman Robert Anderson built the first electric vehicle, powered by a nonrechargeable battery. In 1881, American blacksmith Thomas Davenport invented the first direct-current electric motor and produced the first functional electric vehicle, reaching speeds of 12 km/h. In the 1880s, in step with the modern Western mindset, electric cars became fashionable: they were quiet, smokeless, and required less maintenance than gasoline vehicles. In 1897, Belgian racer Camille Jenatzy became the first person to reach 100 km/h in an electric car.

Yet the popularity of those early EVs—so integral to the modern imagination—waned in the early 1900s as mass production demanded less originality and more efficiency. Charging infrastructure was limited (an issue still "work in progress"), while gasoline cars became ever more efficient and affordable. By 1930, most electric-car production had ceased. The century of oil had begun.

At the turn of the twenty-first century, interest in EVs resurged like a tidal wave—driven by high oil prices, environmental concerns, rapid battery advances, and the climate agenda. But something deeper underlies this boom: a cultural and economic shift that will inevitably consolidate in the coming years and redefine how we live and understand the world.

Today EVs are more efficient and affordable than ever; their batteries have higher capacity, extending driving range, and charging networks have improved. Battery costs have fallen by roughly 80 to 90 percent since 2010, helping electric vehicles move toward mass-market competitiveness. Internal-combustion engines are thermodynamically inefficient, often losing the majority of fuel energy as heat, which highlights the structural efficiency advantage of electric drivetrains. As a result, adoption is accelerating rapidly: in 2024, more than 17 million electric cars were sold worldwide,[12] a figure rising month after month. Infinite Machine's Olto electric scooter extends this same cost-curve logic to urban micro-mobility, using modular, swappable components so that batteries and key parts can be repaired or upgraded rather than replaced, further compressing lifetime ownership costs. A report by Rho Motion, a firm specializing in EV-market analysis, revealed that late in 2023 global sales reached a new monthly record of 1.4 million units, up from 1.1 million the year before.

In 2017, only 1 percent of global car sales were electric. Today that figure has since risen to roughly 25 percent, and EVs are expected to account for more than half of all new-car sales by 2035.

Rho Motion again: In 2024, global sales of battery-electric (BEV) and plug-in hybrid (PHEV) vehicles exceeded 17 million units, up from 13.6 million in 2023. That same year, the United Kingdom's new Zero-Emission Vehicle

[12] International Energy Agency (IEA), *Trends in electric car markets – Global EV Outlook 2025*, https://www.iea.org/reports/global-ev-outlook-2025/trends-in-electric-car-markets-2 (Accessed October 26, 2025).

(ZEV) mandate took effect, requiring that 22 percent of all new cars sold be fully electric—rising to 80 percent by 2030. Manufacturers must therefore convince consumers to keep choosing EVs. The keys? A more attractive lineup, better charging infrastructure, and narrower price gaps.

The International Energy Agency projects that EVs will account for 30 percent of global car sales by 2030 and exceed 60 percent by 2040. Including both BEVs and PHEVs, they could reach 50 percent of new-car sales in the United States by 2030.[13] Because transportation is among the largest industries on earth, this shift will redraw the global economic map—creating vast opportunities for some and losses for others. Success will go to those who embrace both electric and autonomous technologies.

Although fully autonomous vehicles (Levels 4 and 5) are not yet mass-market, the race already has clear contenders. Deployment currently centers on pilot programs and robotaxi fleets in select cities, plus specialized trucking applications.

The Secret of Success

Companies with vertical integration—control over multiple stages of the supply chain—are best positioned to respond quickly to the upheaval sweeping the auto industry.

Another key strategy for competitiveness is improving the efficiency of the electric powertrain: the system of components that generate and transmit the power required to move the car, including the motor, transmission, and related subsystems. In EVs, a large share of battery energy feeds the powertrain, but not all becomes motion. Boosting efficiency is therefore essential to maximize battery use and extend range—critical for mass adoption by millions of drivers accustomed to the instant response of combustion engines.

Energy density in batteries—especially those powering EVs and consumer electronics—is decisive. The path forward involves increasing the nickel content in cathodes and using silicon anodes, two materials that can store far more energy than conventional ones and that will become the building blocks of tomorrow's transport.

Solid-state batteries are progressing from laboratory research into pilot-scale development, with automakers targeting higher energy density and faster charging in the coming years.

[13] *InsideEVs*, "EVs Could Reach 50% Market Share by 2030," January 9, 2025, https://insideevs.com/news/726251/evs-50-percent-market-share-2030/. (Accessed October 26, 2025).

The winners in the auto sector are clearly those that have mastered electric and autonomous technologies. The battery has become the central component, and it is no coincidence that the world's largest EV maker, BYD, was a battery company only a few years ago. Alongside battery producers, cell suppliers, charging-network operators, and software/ADAS developers are also capturing new growth. Vertically integrated manufacturers that moved fast—especially Chinese groups such as BYD and Geely, plus a wave of new OEMs that rapidly scaled BEV output—are dominating. BYD topped global EV sales in 2024[14] with over 4 million units delivered and about 18 percent global market share. Geely sold more than 900,000 EVs (up 92 percent year-on-year) and has been expanding aggressively across Europe.[15] Tesla remains a worldwide leader in brand and technology, with 1.79 million EVs delivered in 2024[16] (around an 11 percent global share), but it has lost ground to lower-cost Chinese competitors.

The losers are legacy automakers that clung to internal-combustion models or moved too slowly on electrification, failing to secure battery capacity and thus ceding market share. Meanwhile, the growth of road-transport oil demand is flattening—a long-term risk for petroleum suppliers—while parts makers tied to combustion-engine chains face shrinking margins. In China, the world's largest EV market, brands like Toyota, Volkswagen, General Motors, Kia, Honda, and Nissan saw combined passenger-car sales fall sharply between 2020 and 2024, while domestic Chinese brands doubled theirs.

What explains the success of EVs? One major driver is the Net-Zero by 2050 scenario[17], which set a global framework for reaching net-zero CO_2 emissions by mid-century. Government support through regulation and subsidies, aimed at cutting pollution, has been, and will remain, crucial.

Public spending on EV incentives and subsidies had already doubled by 2021, with grants covering up to 40 percent of the cost of zero-emission

[14] *CNN*, "China's BYD Annual Sales Pass Tesla," March 25, 2025, https://edition.cnn.com/2025/03/25/cars/china-byd-annual-sales-pass-tesla-intl-hnk (Accessed October 26, 2025).

[15] *Geely Automobile Holdings Limited*, "Geely Automobile Records Revenue and Profit Growth in 2024," March 21, 2025, https://www.geely.com/en/news/2025/geely-automobile-records-revenue-profit-2024 (Accessed October 26, 2025).

[16] *Tesla, Inc.*, "Tesla Fourth Quarter 2024 Production, Deliveries and Deployments," January 29, 2025, https://ir.tesla.com/press-release/tesla-fourth-quarter-2024-production-deliveries-and-deployments. (Accessed October 26, 2025).

[17] *International Energy Agency (IEA), Net Zero by 2050: A Roadmap for the Global Energy Sector*, May 2021, https://www.iea.org/reports/net-zero-by-2050 (Accessed October 26, 2025).

trucks.[18] A growing list of countries has pledged to phase out combustion engines or set ambitious electrification goals for coming decades.

The United States has enacted tougher fuel-efficiency standards and passed the Infrastructure Investment and Jobs Act, which allocates funding for nationwide EV-charging networks. The European Union's CO_2-emission standards for passenger and heavy-duty vehicles promote EV adoption and keep Europe among the most dynamic markets; projections point to EVs surpassing 35 percent of passenger-car sales by 2030.

China, for its part, continues to outperform expectations. In 2024, EV sales growth was led by China, followed by Europe and the U.S. That year China sold 11 million EVs—more than the rest of the world combined. As in most arenas, U.S.–China dynamics combine rivalry and cooperation: China dominates with the world's largest EV market and a booming domestic industry, while the U.S. boasts Tesla's global prominence and rising investment from legacy carmakers. Government policies, technological progress, and trade tensions have all shaped this contest. Tariffs and intellectual-property disputes have caused friction, yet both nations—at least in theory—recognize EVs' environmental benefits. Despite the rivalry, global expansion and future collaboration remain likely as the EV sector evolves.

Meanwhile, many carmakers have electrification plans that go well beyond regulations. About 785 new EV models are currently available worldwide;[19] in 2021 alone there were five times as many as in 2015, greatly increasing consumer visibility and appeal. By 2030, BMW, Volkswagen, and Daimler expect at least 50 percent of their fleets to be electric. The U.S. trump card is the emergence of a truly affordable Tesla. As *Wired* reported in January 2024: "Tesla CEO Elon Musk told investors today that a cheaper Tesla EV will arrive by the end of next year."

In fact, this was part of a master plan Musk unveiled back in 2006:[20]

Our long-term plan is to build a wide range of models, including affordable family cars. Tesla's overarching goal is to accelerate the shift from a mine-and-burn hydrocarbon economy to a solar-electric one. To achieve that, a no-compromise electric car is critical—hence the Tesla Roadster, designed

[18] *International Energy Agency (IEA), Global EV Outlook 2021: Accelerating Ambitions Despite the Pandemic*, April 2021, https://www.iea.org/reports/global-ev-outlook-2021 (Accessed October 26, 2025).

[19] *International Energy Agency (IEA), Global EV Outlook 2025: Trends in the Electric Car Industry*, May 2025, https://www.iea.org/reports/global-ev-outlook-2025/trends-in-the-electric-car-industry (accessed October 26, 2025).

[20] Elon Musk, *"The Secret Tesla Motors Master Plan (Just Between You and Me)," Tesla Blog*, August 2, 2006. Available at: https://www.tesla.com/blog/secret-tesla-motors-master-plan-just-between-you-and-me (Accessed October 27, 2025).

to beat a Porsche or Ferrari in a head-to-head. Some may ask: do we really need another high-performance sports car? Will it change global carbon emissions? The answers are: no, and not much. That's beside the point unless you understand the secret master plan. Every new technology starts with high unit costs, and EVs are no exception. Tesla's strategy is to enter at the high end, where customers can pay a premium, and then move down-market as fast as possible—boosting volume and cutting prices with each successive model.

Yet projections and estimates mean little without the right infrastructure. By 2024 there were over 4.5 million public EV chargers worldwide—evidence that to sustain future sales growth, charging networks must expand severalfold by 2030.

This is no small matter, since it underpins one of EVs' main advantages: charging costs far less than gasoline. Electric cars also require minimal maintenance, are far more efficient, and—thanks to technology, competition, and government incentives—are becoming ever more affordable.

The implication is clear: within a few years, owning an electric car will be more common than owning one powered by gasoline or diesel.

Investment Case Study: Build Your Dreams (BYD) and Geely (175 HK)

> *We believe in on the ground research and in investment teams that were born in the regions in which they invest*

BYD and Geely are poised to dominate the global EV industry. Their vast production scale and manufacturing efficiency give them formidable cost advantages. I am convinced that investors have underestimated their R&D spending, particularly on autonomous-driving technology. Remarkably, both companies offer these advanced features free or at very low cost—unlike Tesla, which charges a premium. This price-and-volume strategy underpins their rapid expansion across multiple markets.

A few years ago, BYD was merely a battery maker. Today it is the world's largest electric-vehicle company—a symbol of the global shift toward electrification and a textbook example of how China leverages scale to conquer new industries.

In early 2024 we added BYD to our model portfolio, expecting it to extend its leadership both in China and abroad. A core element of our thesis was that the world was underestimating—not only BYD's R&D—but also its scale and margin-expansion potential. BYD, for instance, provides autonomous-driving technology free of charge and has achieved five-minute battery charging times. Its growth rests on several structural drivers:

- Vertical integration. Unique among major automakers, BYD controls its supply chain end-to-end—from lithium-ion batteries to semiconductors—ensuring cost stability and margin protection during the volatile raw-material cycle of 2021–2023.

- Cost advantage. Its Blade Battery technology delivers industry-leading safety and efficiency at scale, enabling BYD to sell EVs profitably at price points where rivals lose money or withdraw.
- Export growth. By early 2024, exports to Europe, Latin America, and Southeast Asia were growing triple-digits year-over-year, with the Atto 3 and Dolphin models gaining traction in price-sensitive markets.
- Policy tailwinds. Even as subsidies declined, China continued supporting EVs through charging infrastructure and tax incentives.

By early 2025, Tesla and BYD dominated headlines—but the advantage lay with the Chinese firm, which had already surpassed its American rival in global sales of electric and hybrid vehicles. Geely stood out as another Chinese automaker that had achieved national scale and international credibility, with robust growth and an equity valuation still deeply discounted. We initiated a position in Geely in February 2025.

That same year I visited a Zeekr showroom in Hong Kong—Geely's premium EV brand. At the time, the company's electric-vehicle volume sales were rising 80 percent, overall sales 30 percent. It will not be long before Geely sells more electric cars than Tesla.

The author with a high-end electric vehicle at a Geely dealership in Hong Kong.

To be successful when investing in companies from emerging markets, it is essential to have the right macroeconomic view of the country where you are investing. In the case of China—a major importer of oil and semiconductors—the electric-vehicle (EV) industry is a strategic one. Growth in EVs translates into fewer imports and reduced economic dependence on exporting countries. Thus, as the electric car industry expands, China becomes stronger, both economically and in terms of national security.

Today, China is the largest EV market in the world, accounting for more than 60% of global sales—a situation largely due to the fact that it began developing this technology much earlier than most countries. In this sense, electric vehicles are giving China a position of power in the automotive industry that it did not previously have. This industry is opening the door for China to dominate the global car sector—a space traditionally held by countries like Germany, Japan, the United States, and more recently, South Korea. Now, it is China that is leading the transformation, driven primarily by electric vehicles.

Beyond understanding the macro picture, our investment process focuses on understanding the companies we invest in better than anyone else. We devote around 75% of our analysis to this, which includes identifying the best management teams in each country, assessing the future growth of various industries and companies, and determining which firms have the greatest competitive advantages within their industries—and therefore, which can sustain a high return on invested capital over a long period of time. We also place strong emphasis on understanding companies' corporate governance in detail.

Additionally, we always seek to invest in the global themes or sectors with the highest growth potential over the next ten years. This is the case for BYD and China, for whom electric cars are strategic. That is why the Chinese government has promoted their growth—and will continue to do so. Driven largely by this momentum, there is no doubt that electric vehicles will continue to replace gasoline cars in the coming years.

The Future According to the Jetsons

In the early 1960s, at the height of America's space-age optimism before Apollo 11 and the Moon landing of Neil Armstrong and Edwin E. Aldrin, the Hanna-Barbera studio aired a futuristic animated sitcom set in the distant—yet desirable—year 2062. *The Jetsons* depicted a typical middle-class American family living in a house suspended in the sky. The father worked three hours a day, three days a week; they drove flying cars that looked like tiny saucers; vacationed on *Las Venus*; watched flat-screen TVs and made video calls; ate meals prepared by intelligent appliances; and had both a robot maid and a talking dog. In short, nothing beyond what an ideal family of the future might expect.

First broadcast on ABC during the decade of the Moon landing, *The Jetsons* returned in the 1980s—by then, the dream of space conquest had given way to Cold War rivalry. Today, forty years later, the flying cars once planted in our collective imagination are no longer pure fantasy. Several companies plan to begin producing and marketing them within a few years, and the global urban air mobility market could be worth up to $1.5 trillion by 2040.[21] By 2030, eVTOL aircraft could turn a 90-minute traffic grind into an 8-minute

[21] Morgan Stanley Research, *"Flying Cars: Investment Implications of Autonomous Urban Air Mobility,"* December 2018, https://www.morganstanley.com/ideas/autonomous-aircraft (Accessed October 26, 2025).

sky hop. Over a 40-year career, that kind of daily time saving would add up to nearly three full years of life reclaimed from commuting.

The industry leader is Embraer, the world's third-largest aircraft manufacturer, which is developing an urban air vehicle aptly named Eve. Eve is an electric, vertical take-off and landing aircraft designed to be quiet, energy-efficient, and suitable for short trips of up to 100 km. Its delta-wing design includes eight electric motors and room for four passengers plus one pilot. Embraer plans to commercialize Eve in 2026 and has already received more than 1,200 orders.

By 2035, Embraer projects that the city of Rio de Janeiro will host about 245 urban air vehicles, 37 vertiports (take-off and landing hubs for cargo drones and passenger shuttles), more than 100 air routes, 4.5 million passengers, and roughly USD 220 million in sales, with average fares around USD 48.[22] And Eve is hardly alone: Germany's Volocopter, now operating under new ownership after insolvency proceedings, and the defunct Lilium were also prominent contenders, alongside U.S.-based players such as Joby Aviation and Archer Aviation, are all in development.

Sooner or later, flying cars will revolutionize not just our imagination but our daily mobility. Mass adoption will take time—initially constrained by price, still estimated around 1 million USD depending on capacity, range, and technology—but they will help relieve traffic in major cities and shorten travel times across rural distances.

To measure the impact of this transport revolution purely in quantitative terms would be a case of severe myopia—the chronicle of a foreseen mistake. The most "techno-optimistic" among us envision, in the medium term, virtuous urban networks where scheduled, shared trips integrate seamlessly with today's public transit, cyclists, and pedestrians. The Barcelona Institute for Global Health foresees that "all these characteristics could promote physical activity, reduce air and noise pollution, and create more public space for healthier urban design." Shared autonomous vehicles could significantly reduce the number of privately owned cars in dense urban environments and improve traffic efficiency. While projections vary, higher vehicle utilization and smoother flow could ease congestion and reduce parking demand, potentially freeing up urban land over time.

And while "autonomous" does not necessarily mean "electric," the two will likely converge, further reducing carbon emissions—considering that about 90 percent of transport fuels remain polluting. Shrinking the overall vehicle fleet will benefit both society and the environment, meaning fewer emissions and smoother traffic through cleaner, more efficient technology.

[22] *Embraer S.A.*, *Investor Presentation – May 2023*, May 2023, https://ri.embraer.com.br/en/financial-information/presentations/ (Accessed October 26, 2025).

Ultimately, autonomous vehicles will be inseparable from safer driving. The causes of road accidents are many, but the human factor is constant. Self-driving systems will prevent collisions born of distraction or recklessness. Likewise, in public transit they will shorten waiting times and lower transport costs. Comfortable commuting will turn travel time into productive time—people will read, work, or connect on their laptops and tablets. A car will arrive exactly when we need it, and once our ride ends, it will simply drive away: no parking required.

Reducing driver stress and human error—which contribute to 90 percent of crashes. Shrinking fleets to improve traffic flow and boost total vehicle utilization. Shorter waits, lower fares, smarter intersections thanks to constant vehicle-to-vehicle communication. Less noise, cleaner air. Is that an idealized scenario? Yes—but that doesn't mean it won't define our future. After all, ideals have always propelled humanity's greatest advances. History may be scarred by wars, conflicts, and destruction, but the goal of inventors, visionaries, and entrepreneurs has always been the same: to make the world better.

It is a story being written right now—one that began with the invention of the wheel and has never stopped, because every minute, as you read these words, something new brings us closer to that uncertain yet thrilling and desirable future.

As another visionary—Steve Jobs's successor at Apple, Tim Cook—once said: "Remember when you were a kid, and Christmas Eve was so exciting because you weren't sure what was coming next? Well, it's going to be Christmas Eve for a while."

2

The Materials of the Future

We still do not know one thousandth of one percent of what nature has revealed to us.
Albert Einstein

Across this book's chapters, a vision of the future appears with greater or lesser clarity: a tomorrow that at times seems to promise dramatic change—utopian or dystopian, near or far, sometimes within arm's reach—arriving from the realm of fantasy to our front doors, so that millions of lives may change for the better. The future is alluring; it lets us dream, imagine, and live ahead of time.

When we speak of energy, however, the picture is more complex. Because energy is decisive for our future, it is an urgent matter of the present—pressingly current.

Michael Parfit is a writer, journalist, and filmmaker—and an optimist when it comes to new energy sources. In an article in *National Geographic Magazine*, he sketches a future in which ideas and collaboration are essential, yet even with all hands joined, success is not guaranteed. He writes:

> Practically every energy expert I met did something unexpected: they worked not only in their own specialties but also collaborated in others'. "We will need everything we can get from biomass, everything we can get from solar, everything we can get from wind," says Michael Pacheco, director of the National Bioenergy Center, part of the National Renewable Energy Laboratories in Golden, Colorado. "And the question is: can we get enough?"

The problem is the big numbers. The world uses about 500 billion kilowatt-hours of energy a day. That equals roughly 22 light bulbs burning

P. M. Danziger, *Capital (R)evolution*,
https://doi.org/10.1007/978-3-032-31602-8_2

continuously for every person on the planet. No wonder the glow can be seen from space. Fossil fuels have met growing demand because they pack millions of years of solar energy into a compact form, but we will not find their like again. "If you have a big problem, you must give a big answer," says the energy expert Hermann Scheer, a member of the German Parliament. "If not, people do not believe."

Basilisk, a TU Delft spin-off, has commercialized bio-based self-healing concrete that uses bacteria to seal cracks with limestone when exposed to water. While currently deployed selectively in high-value or durability-critical applications, the technology illustrates how biologically enhanced materials could gradually improve infrastructure longevity and reduce lifecycle maintenance costs over time.

The answers are out there. But they all require one more thing of us—the humans who huddle around the fire of fossil fuels: we will have to take a huge leap... into another kind of world.

Let us step further back, to when no one imagined that "another kind of world" would be necessary. If we look into the last, say, 250 years of history, among many salient facts, there is one we can picture as a staircase everyone ascends and no one descends. The term "industrial revolution" is apt because it captures precisely that: something that came to change everything. And so it did: each industrial revolution served as a hinge, setting productive development and its ad hoc economic model. Alongside this, every revolution had its star element—the brick upon which each empire of modern history was built:

- The First Industrial Revolution, centered chiefly in Great Britain from the late eighteenth to early nineteenth centuries, ran on a strict diet of charcoal.
- The Second Industrial Revolution, straddling the nineteenth and twentieth centuries, added a fossil companion—oil—and harnessed iron to extend the builders' reign towards the skies.
- The Third Revolution—driven by two immaterial goods, information and communication—was more revisionist: by the mid-twentieth century it was imperative to reckon with the consequences and durability of specific energy uses. We began to speak of renewable vs. nonrenewable resources, as even the simplest projections showed gas and oil had an expiry date. New goals followed: employ cleaner energy, store it, and use it efficiently.
- The Fourth Revolution is an explosion born of the third: pure digitalization, as we are witnessing. And the materials that will undergird this "knowledge economy" are copper, lithium, nickel, cobalt, aluminum, graphite, and the so-called "rare earths." These are the materials paving the roads of the coming decades—the materials of the future.

They are, not without reason, called "strategic" minerals and metals, because they are fundamental to low-carbon technologies and thus to national energy transitions, as well as to technologies linked to the digitalization of economies.

These strategic materials are used in electrified vehicles (cobalt, copper, lithium, nickel, and rare earths); batteries (lithium, cobalt, nickel, manganese, and graphite); catalytic converters (platinum, palladium, and rhodium); wind power (aluminum, copper, nickel, and rare earths—more on which below); aeronautics (titanium); and solar photovoltaics (aluminum, silver, copper, and silicon). The metals in a modern battery often travel tens of thousands of kilometers across a globally fragmented supply chain, from mining and refining to cell manufacturing and final assembly, illustrating the strategic and geopolitical complexity of battery production.

Demand and pricing will ebb and flow; doubts and debates will arise. Yet reversal looks unlikely. The path is clear not only because of a cleaner planet: new electricity technologies (solar and wind) are already cheaper than coal-, gas-, or oil-fired power. Electric vehicles are quieter and more agile—as well as cleaner.

All Is History

Let us step back further to recall how we arrived here. That dense black substance we know as coal has a simple origin. As trees and plants died over millennia, their remains accumulated in swamps and lakes; over time and under pressure from the Earth, they became coal. Its virtue lies in the heat it releases when burned. The ancients discovered and used it for warmth and cooking, but its true potential emerged when it powered machinery. In the first Industrial Revolution, coal was the engine of innovation and progress. Mills no longer required water or wind to grind grain. The steam locomotive changed how materials and manufactured goods were transported, extending commercial reach. Where once transport relied on animals and sailing ships, a new world dawned with coal center stage for many decades.

Elmore Leonard's novella *Fire in the Hole* (the seed of the acclaimed TV series *Justified*) is set in small Harlan County, Kentucky, whose economy revolved around an important coal mine. Scarcity condemned the mine to closure, leading to job losses and the degradation of its connected supply chain. The miners' landmark struggles of the 1930s—iconic in US labor history—go unmentioned. What is certain is that shortages have long spurred the search for, or development of, new fuels.

The transition from coal to oil as the principal energy source unfolded mainly in the twentieth century. Oil gained importance as new technologies developed and deposits were discovered worldwide.

The very word *petroleum* has a near-poetic etymology: from Latin *petra* ("rock") and *oleum* ("oil")—"rock oil." Early accounts describe a substance seeping from cracked ground, cave walls, and mines. Although the industry began in the mid-nineteenth century, oil was known in antiquity. The biblical narrative relates that Noah sealed his ark with pitch—a salve made from "rock oil." Mesopotamian peoples traded it in natural or processed form. And it is a key ingredient in the druid Getafix's magic potion, the secret source of power for the indomitable Gauls of Goscinny and Uderzo in *Asterix*.

Oil—calendrical in its precision in shaping the twentieth century—formed from the decomposition of trapped marine microorganisms and plants and transformed by heat and pressure over millennia into a viscous substance. With the invention of the internal-combustion engine, oil propelled cars, aircraft, trains, ships, and even electricity generators. Entire cities grew around refineries; economies were built on production. Its extraction is linked to coal and another key fuel: gas. Nor are oil's uses limited to energy: it is a feedstock for plastics, fertilizers, and chemicals.

The availability of petrol and diesel spurred the mass production of cars and trucks. Thus, a new industry—automotive—was born, rapidly transforming manufacturing, mobility, and logistics. Oil also enabled commercial aviation. First petrol and then kerosene engines allowed longer flights and expanded air routes, connecting regions and countries efficiently.

The shift from coal-fired to oil- and gas-fired power plants improved efficiency and reduced pollution. Electricity generation became more reliable, enabling a broader electrification of society. Looking ahead, oil will likely recede in importance (as coal did before it) yet is unlikely to disappear completely. Indeed, coal still accounts for about 33% of power generation—a nontrivial share.

Oil thus remains fundamental to daily life even as we face the challenge of finding more sustainable energy—*sustainable* because the planet must remain livable and pollution must fall, but also because humanity's consumption volumes require resources that can regenerate. We should not tie our survival to a material that will one day be exhausted. Even so, oil's history is a striking reminder of how a natural resource changed how we live.

A similar story holds for iron. Its discovery marks a milestone: the last period of what we call prehistory. Not a single event, but the widening use of a material that displaced bronze in tools and weapons, shaping civilization in Europe, Asia, and Africa for some three millennia.

Iron is the main ingredient in the recipe for steel—an alloy; we could say steel is iron with a pinch of carbon. That detail is decisive: it confers improved physical and chemical properties.

For a long time, making steel was difficult—and expensive. By the mid-1800s, however, the efforts of Henry Bessemer, Carl Siemens, and Andrew Carnegie bore fruit, and iron could be turned into steel in minutes. That changed everything—again. Cities grew taller thanks to steel-framed skyscrapers, trains ran on rails more durable and easier to bend, and cars became more affordable. And this refers to traditional steel, not the mythic "Rearden metal" with which Ayn Rand built *Atlas Shrugged*.

Thanks to steel, life became more comfortable. It was, in a sense, the foundation stone of our present, ushering in an age of discoveries that transformed the world of the time: oil and gas pipelines, refineries, power stations, transmission lines, assembly lines, skyscrapers, lifts, bridges, reinforced concrete, cars, trucks, buses, trams, railways, aircraft carriers, subways, cranes, bulldozers, tractors, refrigerators, washing machines, dishwashers, nails and screws, clocks, canned food, containers, knives, forks, spoons, and every kind of tool—up to the most iconic superhero of all: the Man of Steel, Superman.

Over the past decade, China has rapidly expanded its role in global EV exports and now anchors much of the battery processing and manufacturing value chain. As the energy transition accelerates, countries rich in critical minerals such as Chile, Indonesia, and the Democratic Republic of the Congo have gained strategic importance, reflecting a structural shift in the geopolitics of energy.

Copper: The Green Superhero

In his *The World Ahead* 2024 trends, Tom Standage, the editor of *The Economist*'s special issue, placed the energy shift front and center (economically and geopolitically) while also noting the polarization it has begun to generate:

> The transition to clean energy is creating new green superpowers and redrawing the map of energy resources. Lithium, copper, and nickel matter much more, while oil and gas—and the regions that dominate their supply—matter less. Competition for green resources is reshaping geopolitics and trade, creating unexpected winners and losers. Meanwhile, a backlash against the green transition is emerging among voters who see climate-friendly policies as an elite-driven agenda against ordinary people.

On screen, superheroes save us from alien invasions, autocratic regimes, revenge-driven villains, and those who are evil for hidden trauma—or simply by choice. Given today's context, we may be closer to needing a superhero to save us from ourselves. Extractivism, pollution, and inadequate waste treatment, among other causes, have driven the search for new materials. Yet for a portion of a polarized public, these superheroes are villains.

Enter copper, a material that rarely sparks controversy, as Parfit put it in his article:

> I am in a messy room, surrounded by the remnants of electronic enthusiasm: wire peelings, bits of copper, connectors, pliers. To me they are the tools of freedom. I have just installed a dozen solar panels on my roof. And they work. A meter shows that 1,285 watts of energy are coming straight from the sun to my system, charging my batteries, cooling my drinks, buzzing in my computer, and freeing my life.

Copper as a path to freedom. It is not only essential to the world economy; it is the new green superhero. Copper is tied to technological development because it is used in products such as electrical wiring, electronic equipment, automobiles, and construction machinery: it is an excellent thermal and electrical conductor. We handle it daily; we can attest to its malleability and strength. It is considered a "green" material—contributing to sustainability—because it can be recycled without losing its properties.

These facts are hardly new. Above we mentioned the Iron Age, the last great technological stage of prehistory. It was preceded by the Bronze Age and, before that, the Copper Age. Hammered copper objects dating to c. 6000 BC have been found, as well as images detailing metal-smelting processes. Given today's extensive uses, we might say we are living through a second Copper Age.

Copper is among the most widely used materials in electronics, power-transmission systems, and telecommunications: it is present in printed circuit boards and connectors in devices such as mobile phones and computers. Copper cables and connections are used in solar PV panel manufacture and energy-storage devices. It also appears in plumbing components and systems thanks to its durability and corrosion resistance; for the same reason, it is used in roofing and cladding. In the automotive industry it is found in radiators and motors because of its heat-dissipation capacity. It forms windings in electric motors and electromagnets due to its conductivity and ability to generate magnetic fields and is used in generators and transformers. A gasoline car contains about 23 kilograms of copper, a battery-electric car about 83 kilograms, and an electric bus nearly 370 kilograms, turning electrification into a copper-intensive transition. In shipbuilding it coats submerged hulls to prevent marine growth. Many cookware items use copper for its thermal conductivity. It is also widely used in coinage and jewelry for its sheen and malleability. Unseen though it may be, copper is everywhere.

Chile is currently the world's leading producer, with roughly 23% of global mine output, followed by the Democratic Republic of Congo and then Peru; together the three account for close to half of world supply.[1]

On the demand side, China is the top consumer, accounting for 50% or more of global demand. This has several implications. China's role significantly affects copper prices, with economic repercussions for producer nations. China is also active in copper-mining operations abroad to secure supply—bringing potential social and environmental consequences for host countries. Moreover, China has developed strong recycling technologies and copper alternatives. Because copper is crucial to renewable-energy technologies, Chinese demand may be pivotal in accelerating the transition to a greener economy.

AI data centers could add close to 1 million tons of incremental copper demand by 2030, an $8–10 billion annual materials surge at current prices. Projected AI-driven data center electricity demand this decade could rise by several hundred terawatt-hours—equivalent to adding the annual electricity consumption of 8–10 countries like Portugal to the global grid.

Summarizing copper's importance, a Faster Capital report highlighted its star qualities:

1. Solar power generation. Used in PV panels to convert sunlight efficiently into electricity; PV cells contain thin copper layers that conduct generated electricity.
2. Wind power generation. Turbines rely on copper for components and wiring; its conductivity enables efficient transmission from generator to grid. Durability and corrosion resistance make it ideal for turbine cabling.
3. Energy storage. Owing to its stability and reliability, copper is widely used in storage technologies such as batteries and supercapacitors—for example, as foils and conductors in battery electrodes.
4. Electric vehicles. The rise of EVs as a sustainable alternative to ICE vehicles has further increased copper demand.

[1] Informe Tendencias del Mercado del Cobre. Primer trimestre de 2023. Comisión Chilena del Cobre (COCHILCO).

For the same reason, experts expect copper demand to grow in developing countries (and note: more economic growth implies more urbanization, more consumption—more of everything). Global copper demand could reach c. 36 Mt in 2031, up from roughly 25.5 Mt in 2023. The main drivers are EVs and electrification (a topic addressed in another chapter).

Not all that glitters is copper, however. A key notion here is material intensity—the quantity of a given material used across a product's life cycle. The US Department of Energy considers copper's material intensity to be very high for both standard vehicles and electric cars and buses.[2] In the medium term, projected demand would outstrip available supply: a medium supply risk. In the US case, this risk stems from rising demand linked to renewables and electrification. Other factors also weigh: permitting to open new mines or expand existing ones is stricter, with a focus on environmental stewardship and community protection. An additional constraint: not all reserves are easily accessible or economically viable, which could yield lower-than-expected volumes.

Despite these issues, US miner Freeport-McMoRan notes that the global copper market remains buoyant: electrification is expanding rapidly thanks to advances in alternative energy and EV production. There is a growing—and positive—consensus about copper's future, with demand expected to grow faster than supply. In short, copper shines in an ever more electrified world.[3]

Investment Case Study: Freeport-McMoRan (FCX)

> *We invest in companies that have good corporate governance, and particularly in companies in which the majority shareholders are aligned with the minority shareholders.*

Freeport-McMoRan (FCX) is one of the world's largest producers of copper and gold, with an annual output of approximately 4.0 billion lb of copper (≈1.8 Mt), 1.6 million oz of gold, and c. 80 million lb of molybdenum.

The company operates large-scale, long-life assets in Indonesia (≈40% of copper sales), South America (≈27%), and the United States (≈33%), according to its 2025–2027 mid-term production outlook, which incorporates growth from its new Indonesian smelter, the Bagdad and El Abra brownfield projects, and the expansion of its US leaching program.

[2] U.S. Department of Energy, Critical Materials Assessment, 2023.

[3] Freeport-McMoRan Inc., Second-Quarter and Six-Month 2023 Results, July 20, 2023. Available at: https://investors.fcx.com/investors/news-releases/news-release-details/2023/Freeport-McMoRan-Reports-Second-Quarter-And-Six-Month-2023-Results/default.aspx (Accessed October 2025).

Over the long run, winning commodity producers are clearly those with the lowest marginal production costs—and those able to grow volumes at low marginal cost. Because the product is largely undifferentiated, competitive advantage lies in producing more cheaply. Low-cost firms can endure longer when prices are depressed and earn more when prices are high. Freeport operates a very low-cost copper mine in Indonesia, and costs should fall further as production there grows.

Investing in commodity producers requires understanding cyclicality: high fixed costs (to build and maintain a mine) and volatile selling prices. For cyclicals, we want to invest when margins are low and an inflection point is near—typically when the commodity's price has favorable prospects.

Our investment process captures this well: getting the macro view right—in these cases, the commodity-price view—is vital. We also consider entry timing crucial; even with the right company, an entry point can materially alter returns. For cyclicals, timing matters even more.

Corporate governance is another key point when investing in equities. Majority and minority shareholders should be well aligned. Social and environmental policy is important, especially in materials producers like Freeport; lapses can cause pollution or flooding, triggering heavy fines or shutdowns. Absent clear social and environmental policy, the risks of workplace fatalities and reputational damage also rise.

We initiated an investment in Freeport-McMoRan on September 26, 2025. We view it as a good entry point: the share price overreacted when the company announced a temporary halt at certain Indonesian operations following an accident at one of its mines. While restoration will take time, we believe operations will resume and see attractive growth in Indonesia with low marginal costs. We often observe such overreactions in commodity stocks upon mine-related headlines. Our process places heavy emphasis on incorporating market-behavior biases; fear and uncertainty create powerful skews. Because our analyst team includes people born in the regions where we invest, because we have researched the same companies for twenty years, and because we have direct access to management of companies, we can analyze each situation quickly and deeply to judge whether the market is overreacting.

Cobalt Blue: The Oxygen of Technology

Lithium has long been touted as central to technological progress—rightly so. We address it below, but first pause on other protagonists of the digital leap. Like lithium, cobalt is essential in many batteries used in EVs, phones, and computers. This blue metal helps batteries store very large amounts of energy while keeping temperatures stable in both extremes of cold and heat, making it useful in aerospace, defense, and medical applications as well as a key element in clean-energy technologies. It also contributes to the performance of lithium-ion batteries, which, unlike common household cells, can be recharged and reused for years (though they are more expensive and harder to recycle).

Cobalt is a byproduct of copper and nickel extraction, occurring naturally in those deposits. Given rising interest, mining operations focused specifically on cobalt are being developed to meet growing demand, especially for lithium-ion batteries in EVs and electronic devices.

Countries with the largest cobalt reserves include the Democratic Republic of Congo (DRC), Australia, Indonesia, the Philippines, and Russia. Production growth is concentrated mainly in DRC and Indonesia, with new mining and processing projects. The DRC is the principal source of mined cobalt, at around 70% of global output. China is the top producer of refined cobalt, largely from semi-processed cobalt imported from the DRC. Canada, Australia, and Russia also produce significant volumes.

Cobalt now sits at the heart of the energy and technology revolution. According to the World Economic Forum, battery-related cobalt demand is expected to quadruple by 2030—driven largely by widespread EV adoption.

Expansion in cobalt production across emerging countries brings challenges—from the investment needed to develop new mines and processing plants to the complex, costly technology required to extract and process cobalt efficiently. A fundamental concern is working conditions in artisanal mines, which trended on TikTok during 2023. Between 15% and 30% of the DRC's cobalt comes from "artisanal" mines where thousands work in "inhuman," "degrading" conditions, according to Siddharth Kara of Harvard's T.H. Chan School of Public Health. Kara, who has researched modern slavery, human trafficking, and child labor for years, describes in *Cobalt Red: How the Blood of the Congo Powers Our Lives* how the "cobalt rush" has caused countless deaths and widespread contamination of water, soil, and air near mines.

Aluminum and Nickel: Body and Soul of Electric Vehicles

Aluminum needs little introduction. Ubiquitous in modern construction, it does not send us running for a periodic table. Because it is light, corrosion-resistant, and malleable, it is used to build all kinds of structures—telecom towers, antennas, and power networks. It is also highly recyclable, making it an environmentally sustainable choice. Aluminum features in batteries, wiring, and circuits. Solar panels, wind turbines, and batteries require aluminum. In aircraft it is used in structure, wings, and fuselage; in ships, in structure, hull, and engines; in cars, in bodywork, chassis, and engine components; and in electronic devices, in housings, components, and connectors.

Today it is central to EV manufacture, driving higher demand.[4] All projections point to rising production, enriched by high recycled content. One illustration: aluminum demand for EVs and solar is estimated at 16 Mt by 2029 (EVs may require up to 250 kg of aluminum per unit—three times that of ICE vehicles).

Countries with the largest bauxite reserves (aluminum's ore) are Guinea, Australia, Vietnam, Brazil, and Jamaica. Major aluminum producers include China, India, Russia, Canada, the United Arab Emirates, Australia, and Bahrain. Many are also major consumers: China, the United States, India, Japan, Germany, South Korea, Brazil, and Russia. These already large numbers sum to eight-figure totals that confirm aluminum's privileged place in industry.

Nickel's story is a fascinating saga spanning centuries. Discovered in Europe in the eighteenth century, it takes its name from the German *Kupfernickel*—"the devil's copper"—because miners struggled to extract copper from nickel-bearing ore. Despite that inauspicious start, nickel gained value over time. It was used as a coating to protect iron and steel from corrosion and in coinage (hence its English common name). With the Industrial Revolution, it became more important for its properties in industry. Demand rose considerably with the production of stainless steel and other heat- and chemical-resistant alloys.

In the late nineteenth century, large deposits were discovered in Canada, contributing to global supply. Today nickel is essential in a wide range of industrial and technological applications. Its industrial value lies not only in its physical characteristics but also in its chemistry: it readily alloys with many metals in varied proportions to deliver diverse results. It is employed in stainless steel (corrosion-resistant) used in buildings, bridges, and industrial equipment; as a catalyst in many chemical reactions, including oil hydrogenation and chemical production; in rechargeable Ni-Cd and Ni-MH batteries for devices such as cordless phones and digital cameras; in high-strength superalloys for aircraft and rocket engine components requiring high-temperature and corrosion resistance; and in electroplating, applying a nickel layer to protect other metals. Stainless-steel cookware is popular owing to corrosion resistance; nickel is essential in these alloys. Nickel is also used in energy-sector tubing and piping to transport corrosive liquids and

[4] "Aluminum Market by Technavio." PR Newswire, April 22, 2022.

gases at high temperatures and pressures; in cast parts and electrical steel for automotive, industrial machinery, and electronics; in precious-metal alloys (e.g., silver, white gold) to improve jewelry strength and durability; in electronics, where printed circuit boards are nickel-plated; in nuclear-reactor components; and in medical devices and prostheses thanks to corrosion resistance and biocompatibility.

In recent years, nickel sulfate demand has grown extraordinarily due to its essential role in the EV mobility and energy-storage revolution. EV nickel demand could climb sharply by 2030—from ~700,000 t to ~2,300,000 t. Prices may also rise on both demand and scarcity—an understandable concern.

Top nickel producers include Indonesia, the Philippines, Russia, and New Caledonia; the largest reserves are in Indonesia, Australia, Brazil, Russia, and New Caledonia. Production could become more concentrated in fewer countries—Indonesia and Russia—poised to be pivotal market actors. Suppliers will be under pressure to reduce environmental impacts. Will this drive new low-emission nickel-production technologies? Suppliers will have to adapt to market—and environmental—challenges to remain competitive.

In EVs, solutions generate paradoxical problems: according to a sustainability report by Kearney for automakers Polestar and Rivian, EV supply chains emit up to 50% more greenhouse gases than those for ICE vehicles, with batteries accounting for nearly a third of total emissions. Even so, *Reuters* notes: "None of this should dampen climate-minded investors' enthusiasm for the EV boom. According to researchers at the University of Michigan, after about 30,000 km, the cumulative emissions (including production) of an EV are far lower than those of a gas guzzler."

Lithium: The Magic Metal

Imagine a world in which silent, zero-emission vehicles replace roaring, smoking combustion engines. When we reach that point—within this twenty-first century—it will be thanks to lithium. The "magic metal" at the heart of batteries has unleashed a revolution in electric mobility. Electric cars, scooters, and bikes have become common on our streets. A typical electric-vehicle battery uses 5,000 to 10,000 times more lithium than a smartphone. But lithium's impact goes far beyond mobility. It has shrunk our electronics, letting us carry everything from smartphones to ultrathin laptops with ease. Lithium has made technology more portable and accessible than ever. It also underpins our transition to cleaner energy: it stores electricity generated by sun and wind, helping homes and businesses run on renewables even when clouds gather or winds calm. Expect to see appliances and power tools running on lithium batteries. Most fascinating of all, the quest for better lithium batteries is driving global innovation. Chemists and materials scientists are working tirelessly on batteries that are more efficient, longer-lasting, and safer—spurring advances in robotics, AI, and beyond.

Lithium's history spans two centuries. Discovered by Johan August Arfwedson in 1817 and isolated as a metal four years later by William Thomas Brande, it saw early use in ceramics, glass, and even nascent medicine. Its true revolution arrived in the 1990s, when Sony commercialized the first lithium-ion batteries for consumer electronics. In this century, lithium became essential in EV and stationary-storage batteries, boosting extraction and production worldwide.

All signs point to rising demand in coming years, potentially driving higher prices and greater competition. Supply contests often conceal deeper geopolitical competition, as potential conflicts could emerge over lithium deposits concentrated in a few territories. The leading producers are Australia, Chile, China, and Argentina, while Bolivia, Argentina, Chile, Australia, and China hold the largest identified resources. However, in terms of proven economic reserves, Australia and Chile clearly dominate global supply. This geographic concentration—both in extraction and processing—heightens the risk of strategic tension among producing countries and industrial powers, as each seeks to secure stable access to this critical mineral. Global lithium demand was ≈920,000 t LCE in 2023 (≈140,000 t Li in batteries alone) and could rise to ≈2.0–2.5 million t LCE by 2030—with high scenarios above 3 million—driven by EVs and BESS (Battery Energy Storage Systems).

"Rare Earths," or Hidden Jewels

In a corner of the periodic table where chemistry grows more mysterious lies a group known as the "rare earths" or rare-earth elements (REEs). Though thought of as rare, they are not especially scarce; the name reflects the historical difficulty of isolating and studying them. They also typically occur at low concentrations and across different minerals, complicating extraction. Our journey through rare earths runs across the eighteenth and nineteenth centuries, when intrepid scientists worldwide searched for and isolated them. Cerium, lanthanum, and praseodymium were among the first discovered. Their names tell intriguing stories too: *lanthanum* derives from Greek *lanthanein*, "to lie hidden," because in nature it is not readily accessible.

The seventeen rare earths are lanthanum, cerium, praseodymium, neodymium, promethium, samarium, europium, gadolinium, terbium, dysprosium, holmium, erbium, thulium, ytterbium, lutetium, scandium, and yttrium.

By the twentieth century, rare earths had become key industrial actors. Their versatility and unique properties made them indispensable in electronics, catalysts, permanent magnets and fluorescent lamps. Today they play starring roles in daily life—from the displays on our devices to the magnets that drive electric motors. They are also at the epicenter of the clean-energy revolution, powering wind turbines and solar panels.

Consider the high-definition screens of our devices, from TVs to smartphones: rare earths such as europium and terbium produce their vibrant colors. In clean-energy technologies, rare earths are discreet yet essential heroes—fortifying wind turbines against corrosion and aiding the conversion of sunlight to electricity.

EVs rely on high-performance batteries; and electric motors. Lanthanum is used in the nickel-metal-hydride batteries found in many hybrid vehicles, while neodymium and, in some designs, dysprosium are used in the permanent magnets that power electric traction motors. In lighting, compact fluorescents and high-pressure sodium lamps owe much to rare earths. In chemicals, they are catalytic magicians, accelerating reactions and boosting efficiency in chemical and petrochemical production. In medicine, they enhance MRI imaging and are used in radiotherapy to fight cancer. In defense and security, rare earths silently underpin military communications and the sensor technologies that protect borders.

The rare-earths market is set to grow strongly over the next decade, propelled by clean-tech demand and the electrification of transport and power. Yet, as with lithium, production concentrated in a few countries poses supply-security challenges—underlining the need for recycling and sustainability strategies.

Demand for rare-earth oxides, which reached 196,000 t in 2023, is estimated to rise to 260,000 t by 2030.[5] Annual global demand for neodymium and dysprosium oxides is forecast to substantially exceed annual production by 2030—depleting historically accumulated inventories and ultimately

[5] Alistair MacDonald, "The U.S. Wants a Rare-Earths Supply Chain. Here's Why It Won't Come Easily," *The Wall Street Journal*, April 25, 2023. Available at: https://www.wsj.com/articles/the-u-s-wants-a-rare-earths-supply-chain-heres-why-it-wont-come-easily-dfc3b632 (Accessed October 2025).

causing shortages of these critical magnet materials unless new sources are developed. By 2030, the projected shortfall is ~10,000 t for neodymium and ~400 t for dysprosium.

Countries with the largest reserves[6] include China, Vietnam, Brazil, Russia and India, while the top producers are China, the United States, Australia and Myanmar. China dominates global rare-earth and other strategic material production, conferring significant power and influence in international relations. Smartphones contain more than a dozen rare earth elements, and over 80 percent of global refining capacity for these materials is concentrated in China, creating a structural geopolitical dependency. Australia is a notable producer and has sought to diversify global supply to reduce reliance on China. The United States holds significant reserves but has a comparatively limited production base, prompting efforts to revive domestic industry. Russia, Brazil, and several African countries also have significant reserves, though their current impact on global markets is more limited.

On the map of materials producers and consumers, no nation appears ready to lunge as easily as in board games; this is not *Monopoly*, *The Settlers of Catan*, or *TEG*. China is showing its cards, and everyone knows it holds a strong hand. China is by far the world's largest commodity consumer and a global leader in producing some materials, giving it substantial geopolitical and economic sway. It has invested heavily in mining across Africa and Latin America to secure supplies of the most critical materials.

The figures circulating amid the COVID-19 pandemic were breathtaking. A report by the Rosario Board of Trade (Argentina) surveyed late-2020 data: "Imports in certain categories are at record levels despite the pandemic. There is a generalized increase across all commodities—including minerals, metals and fuels (coal, cobalt, iron ore, oil)—and across many food products."

Emerging markets will continue to play major roles in producing and supplying the materials of the future. Chile and Peru are rich in copper, vital for EVs and renewables. The DRC is a major cobalt producer, crucial for lithium-ion batteries. India and Brazil have significant bauxite reserves, the main source of aluminum. Indonesia is a leading nickel producer—another key high-capacity battery element. While China dominates, Brazil also holds important graphite reserves. As for rare earths, though concentrated mainly in China, Brazil and Vietnam also have untapped potential. The "lithium triangle" (Argentina, Bolivia, and Chile) holds over half of global reserves—yet the processing company supply chain is dominated by China.

[6] U.S. Geological Survey, Mineral Commodity Summaries 2023.

Countries with access to these resources could become new economic powers. Their importance to technology will be a key point in redefining geopolitical alliances, with nations turning to strategic partnerships to secure resources. In the not-too-distant future we will see how the map of future-materials producers is reconfigured—and what strategies they adopt to manufacture them. Countries must prepare for the changes this technology-led order will bring.

In any case, the quest will lie at the intersection of discovering and developing the next fuels—those that let us keep writing humanity's story—and exploiting them responsibly and sustainably. Martin Hoffert, a pioneer in warning about climate-change effects, advances a hypothesis that sounds extreme yet has implacable logic: he believes standing correctly at that crossroads—between exploration/exploitation and responsibility—is more important than (attention!) the war on terror. His reasoning: "Terrorism does not threaten the viability of our high-technology way of life. Energy does."

3

The Energies That Move the World

"A nation that destroys its soils destroys itself."

Franklin D. Roosevelt

Around 1,500 BCE, when the chariots of Ahmose I—the first pharaoh of Egypt's Eighteenth Dynasty—had brought the land under the rule of Thebes, the concentration of carbon dioxide (CO_2) in Earth's atmosphere stood at about 277 parts per million (ppm). When Gautama Buddha attained enlightenment under the Bodhi tree a millennium later, and when Socrates drained his cup of hemlock a century after that, CO_2 levels had barely changed. The same was true when China's Tang Dynasty and the first Islamic Caliphate arose in the seventh century CE and when the Aztec Empire fell to the conquistadors centuries later, halfway across the world. For most of human history, the composition of the planet's atmosphere remained an immutable backdrop to the human drama.

By the mid-nineteenth century, this changed. From a historical perspective, CO_2 levels began to rise abruptly—and from a geological perspective, instantaneously. After remaining between 275 and 285 ppm for millennia, they reached 300 ppm by the 1910s and 412 ppm by 2020. In a single century, a fundamental component of Earth's operating system had shifted a hundred times more rapidly than in the previous thousand years. Global energy consumption today is more than 20 times higher than in 1900, meaning the modern economy runs on an energy scale unprecedented in human history.

So began a special 2021 issue of *The Economist* titled "In Search of Stability," devoted to the challenges and possible solutions surrounding climate change. The topic was hardly new. Yet, after many years—so many that we can now

P. M. Danziger, *Capital (R)evolution*,
https://doi.org/10.1007/978-3-032-31602-8_3

speak in decades—it continues to shape every conversation, projection, and speculation about the future. "Betting that science is wrong and the oil companies are right is by far the dumbest experiment in history." Those are not the words of Greta Thunberg but of one of the most innovative figures of recent decades, Elon Musk. "Sustainable development is a fundamental rupture that will reorganize the entire game. The companies that dominate the future will be those that understand this." Nor is that Greenpeace speaking, but François-Henri Pinault, one of the world's wealthiest and most influential business leaders. Roughly three-quarters of global greenhouse-gas emissions originate in the energy sector; effectively, the same system that fuels modern prosperity sits at the core of the climate equation.

What, precisely, are we talking about? In short, the electrification of the planet is already a fact. Electricity is becoming the central energy source of the global economy. Over the next two decades, hundreds of millions of electric and autonomous vehicles will circulate through cities, while artificial intelligence will demand colossal amounts of electricity to sustain its computing power. At the same time, the share of fossil fuels in the world's energy mix will decline, and renewable sources—chiefly solar and wind—will for the first time exceed 50 percent of global electricity generation by 2035. The result will be a world in which cleaner electricity not only reduces emissions but also enables previously unthinkable uses: autonomous mobility at scale, electrified heavy industry, and the cognitive infrastructure that powers artificial intelligence itself.

Everything Changes—Including the Climate

Why does everyone talk about climate change? Is it a subject placed at the center of the global agenda by environmental movements, or truly the phenomenon with the most inescapable consequences for our lives in the coming years? And, at bottom, is it something entirely new—or merely the most critical stage in a centuries-long evolution of how we live on, and relate to, our planet, bringing humanity to the threshold of a historic transformation, with all the costs and benefits that any structural change entails? To trace the thread, let us travel back to the more recent past.

In the nineteenth century—the century that completed the economic and social revolution of the West and launched us into modernity—traditional biomass was the main source of energy. This consisted primarily of wood but also included crops, alcohol fuels, landfill gas, and refuse: in short, an unsustainable form of energy. Later, the use of coal rose sharply. Coal produced more energy per unit of mass than wood and could be mined in places where timber was scarce. Coal mining expanded during the Industrial Revolution, becoming the primary energy source for industry and transportation from the eighteenth century through the 1950s. Today, that once-promising material—on which we built the foundations of modern life—is among the main generators of carbon dioxide on Earth. Yet it is not alone.

Let us move to Titusville, Pennsylvania, where in 1859 the modern (that is, American) oil boom began, when a steam-powered drill struck the first large-scale commercial oil well. A century later, by 1964, oil had overtaken coal as the world's leading energy source. Economically, oil offered superior performance, storage, and transport advantages: being liquid, it contained roughly twice as much energy per kilogram as coal and was ideally suited for transport.

History repeated itself: a new energy source changed life on the planet. And just as coal had its golden age—when it seemed destined to reign forever—only to be supplanted by oil, so today the "black gold" that shaped and constrained the twentieth century sees its own empire giving way to a new one: the empire of renewables. Unlike their predecessors, these energies do not deplete Earth's nonrenewable resources. They are building the pathways to confront climate change—but they are also much more than that. They are the pillars of a profound transformation in our way of life, the spearhead of a new economic, social, cultural, and political paradigm whose effects we are only beginning to feel.

There is broad scientific, political, and economic consensus (despite a few loud dissenting voices) on the definition of climate change: there is no doubt that the average concentration of greenhouse gases (GHGs) in Earth's atmosphere rose exponentially during the twentieth century and into the twenty-first. This increase is synonymous with ever more frequent and severe natural disasters worldwide—from droughts and wildfires to hurricanes and floods. That is the core of the diagnosis.

Let us return to the origin—to the so-called greenhouse effect. In reality, this effect is simply a set of energy flows moving back and forth between the atmosphere and the planet's surface. The circuit is straightforward: the Earth's surface, warmed by the sun, emits heat as thermal radiation; atmospheric gases absorb part of that radiation and send some of the energy back to Earth's surface. These gases—water vapor, carbon dioxide, nitrous oxide, methane, and others such as hydrofluorocarbons, perfluorocarbons, and sulfur hexafluoride—perform an essential and not inherently harmful function. The problem arises when their concentration rises or falls out of balance.

The greenhouse effect itself is not bad; it is a natural phenomenon that maintains the equilibrium of ecosystems. Its Achilles' heel lies in a beautiful Latin word: equilibrium—or rather, its absence.

The numbers are telling. Between 1980 and 2009, between one-quarter and one-half of Earth's vegetated surface became noticeably greener. Plants thrived in CO_2-enriched air, adding billions of tons of biomass to the planet. The oceans, meanwhile, have become more acidic as they absorbed part of the excess atmospheric CO_2. Carbon dioxide absorbs infrared radiation that would otherwise escape to space, reducing Earth's ability to cool. Higher concentrations of CO_2 intensify this greenhouse effect, leading to a warmer planet. In 2024, global average surface temperature was about 1.55°C above late nineteenth-century levels, marking the first calendar year likely to exceed 1.5°C. To keep global warming below 1.5°C—the golden threshold for maintaining a habitable planet—emissions would need to fall by around 45 percent by 2030 (that is, immediately) and reach net-zero by 2050. Is that achievable, or are we doomed?

To approach an answer, we must go back to the origin of the origin. The main culprit behind the surge in carbon-dioxide emissions is the energy sector: electricity generation, transportation, and industrial use together account for roughly 75 percent of global greenhouse-gas emissions. These three activities are therefore both the target and the solution: transportation, as seen in a previous chapter, through electric vehicles; industry, through large-scale clean technologies; and electricity generation, as explored here, through the now-celebrated and promising renewable energies.

Instructions for Cleaning a Coal Stain

In 2015, the United Nations convened world leaders to seek concrete solutions and move toward a low-carbon global economy. The participants signed a document now familiar to all—the Paris Agreement—committing themselves to reduce greenhouse-gas emissions in order to limit the rise in global temperature this century. A total of 193 countries, plus the European Union, have joined this global initiative, which has since undergone multiple revisions and reinterpretations. On the horizon stand two defining numbers: 2050 and net-zero.

This goal is difficult to reach because it requires sustained cooperation among three actors who rarely manage to work together for long: governments, corporations, and citizens. It is, indeed, a long road, full of obstacles and reversals—but one that is very hard to stop. For this time, it is not the usual bureaucratic exercise in international cooperation whose benefits are invisible to ordinary people. This time, collaboration is essential for everyone—for the average citizen to lead a normal life, for companies to continue producing and selling, and for nations to remain relatively stable.

The countries that signed the Paris Agreement share a common commitment, yet their contributions to climate-change mitigation necessarily reflect national circumstances. Not all bear the same degree of responsibility: the largest emitters of carbon dioxide are the most industrialized nations. A glance at the global economic hierarchy reveals why these same countries dominate this other ranking. The United States, the European Union, and China together account for roughly 60 to 65 percent of the world economy[1] and they top the list of major emitters. The reason is clear: they generate (and consume) more electricity, possess more developed (and intensive) transport systems, and operate larger industries.

For this reason, developing countries insist that industrialized nations must lead emission reductions and provide financial and technological assistance for adaptation and mitigation efforts in poorer economies. They also argue, reasonably, that they too have the right to pursue economic and social development to improve their citizens' quality of life. Energy is essential to that goal, and it can be difficult for these nations to commit to strict reduction targets if doing so limits their opportunities for progress.

The argument is understandable—but it also risks overlooking the opportunity embedded in the challenge. Emerging markets represent 62 percent of the world's population and 48 percent of global emissions.[2] If, over the next decade, they were to concentrate investment in "green" sectors—renewable energy, energy efficiency, electrification, carbon capture and utilization, and low-emission fuels—they could generate more than US $10 trillion in business opportunities, create over 200 million direct jobs, and reduce emissions by around 4 billion tons of carbon dioxide.[3]

[1] International Monetary Fund (IMF), World Economic Outlook (WEO) DataMapper: "Real GDP Growth – Annual % Change (NGDP_RPCH)", Advanced Economies, World, OEMDC/ADVEC/WEOWORLD https://www.imf.org/external/datamapper/NGDP_RPCH@WEO/OEMDC/ADVEC/WEOWORLD/ (Accessed October 27, 2025).

[2] International Finance Corporation (IFC), Climate Investment Opportunities in Emerging Markets: An IFC Analysis (Washington, DC: IFC, December 2016), available at https://www.ifc.org/content/dam/ifc/doc/mgrt/3503-ifc-climate-investment-opportunity-report-dec-final.pdf (Accessed October 27, 2025).

[3] International Finance Corporation (IFC), "Supporting a Green Post-COVID Recovery Can Generate Over USD 10 Trillion in Investment Opportunities in Emerging Markets, Says New IFC Report," January 13, 2021, https://www.ifc.org/en/pressroom/2021/supporting-a-green-post-covid-recovery-can-generate-over-10-trillion-in-investment-opportunities-in-emerging-markets-says-new-ifc-report (accessed October 27, 2025).

The difficulty lies in the fact that this horizon cannot be reached through governmental goodwill alone. Real change requires the combined effort of governments, companies, and individuals. That makes it complex, certainly long-term, but irreversible, because the scale of what is at stake is historic. As the extraordinary British naturalist Sir David Attenborough observed, "For the first time in the history of Homo sapiens, we are asking people of different cultures, on different continents, with different moral systems, to agree. That has never happened in human history. We cannot assume it will happen overnight. We have to keep working at it."

We witness this every day. Community pressure—and, more importantly, the structural need for change—is increasingly influencing both corporations and governments. This is evident not only in legislation favoring green-energy firms but also in the taxes imposed on organizations that fail to meet clean-energy standards. More than forty countries have already adopted some form of carbon pricing, either through direct taxes on fossil fuels or via cap-and-trade systems. In the United Kingdom, coal use plummeted after the introduction of a carbon tax in 2013. In the northeastern United States, nine states have capped emissions from the power sector and require companies to purchase tradable pollution permits.

"Climate change has become a defining factor in companies' long-term prospects.... Awareness is rapidly changing, and I believe we are on the edge of a fundamental reshaping of finance," declared Larry Fink, CEO of BlackRock. "When we see companies not moving with sufficient speed and urgency, our most frequent action will be to hold directors accountable by voting against their re-election."

Energy Is in the Air

As a previous chapter discussed electric vehicles as a solution to fossil-fuel use in transport, here we examine what alternatives renewables present for the power sector—specifically, how and when coal-fired generation will be replaced by thousands of gigawatts from solar and wind. This pathway intersects with another, no less ambitious route: an electrification based on renewable energies (solar, wind, hydropower, and geothermal) that will replace electricity generated from fossil fuels (oil, gas, and coal). Will this be a process that installs itself definitively, changing the landscape overnight like the revolutions of the past? Or are we witnessing a quieter—yet equally or more durable—revolution, in which each step forward, however modest, is irreversible? As Neil Armstrong might say again: one small step for a person, one giant leap for humanity.

Consider how our daily lives would change: moving from an internal-combustion vehicle to one powered by electricity—and retooling production processes within automakers to build them—or replacing a natural-gas heating system with one based on rooftop solar and batteries. Scale up that logic to a neighborhood, or to the construction of a mega-building. Add other facets to this "green composition": waste collection and treatment, recycling, better use of natural light, and water stewardship. Is this a lot or a little? More importantly, is it feasible? Profound change can seem unfathomable—until we bring it into our daily routines and suddenly understand, by identifying with something concrete and simple, just how possible change is.

On the road to decarbonization, renewables are the common bet across sectors. Their advantages are clear: they are the best tool to fight climate change; they are clean and increasingly inexpensive; they draw on virtuous, inexhaustible natural resources; they emit little or no greenhouse gas; they are readily available and, barring extremes, cheaper than coal, oil, or gas. Solar power, for example, is already the cheapest source of new utility-scale electricity in many parts of the United States. The sun is inexhaustible and effortless to harvest, whereas oil and gas are finite and must be extracted and processed to serve as energy. Dependence on natural phenomena could be a drawback, but specialists are working to ensure it is not a weakness.

Caltech's MAPLE experiment demonstrated the feasibility of wirelessly transmitting solar power in space, marking a proof of concept for space-based energy systems. While far from commercial scale, the research suggests a long-term pathway toward continuous, weather-independent solar power if engineering and economic hurdles can be overcome.

Accordingly, wind and solar generation will expand significantly over the coming decades. The cost of solar panels has fallen markedly in the past ten years. By contrast, coal-fired generation is both responsible for a large share of CO_2 emissions and increasingly costly. It is no accident that Abraham Lincoln, in a sense, foresaw wind's power: "As yet, the wind is an untamed and unharnessed force, and quite possibly one of the greatest discoveries hereafter to be made will be the taming and harnessing of it."

Total installed wind and solar photovoltaic capacity is on track to overtake gas and coal. Over the next decade, they will account for a large share of power production. Wind and solar already exceed 13% of global electricity generation, producing roughly 4,000 TWh in 2023,[4] and renewables are projected

[4] Simon Evans and Verner Viisainen, "Analysis: Wind and Solar Added More to Global Energy than Any Other Source in 2023," Carbon Brief, June 20, 2024, https://www.carbonbrief.org/analy

to reach around a 55% share by 2035. Together, wind and solar represented about 97.5% of net capacity additions in 2024. These technologies added 565 GW of capacity in 2024,[5] up from 77 GW in 2012. Steep cost declines have driven this massive growth: between 2010 and 2022, the levelized cost of electricity (LCOE) for solar PV fell by nearly 90%, and for onshore wind by around 70%,[6] attracting a wave of investment. Technological advances are yielding more efficient panels and turbines. As demand for solar products rises, competition lowers material and installation costs while improving manufacturing efficiency. Notably, Chinese turbine manufacturers often operate with costs 30–40% below European and US peers,[7] thanks to highly integrated domestic supply chains, lower labor costs, state support, economies of scale, and intense domestic competition.[8]

Yet the future we are building is not only about substituting one set of sources for another; it is also about how we use and store these new energies. Can renewable energy be conserved and stored? At COP28, held in 2023 in Dubai, energy efficiency was center stage. There—after UN Secretary-General António Guterres stated bluntly that "the phase-out of fossil fuels is inevitable"—participants endorsed a "global pledge on renewables and energy efficiency" to triple installed renewable capacity by 2030 and to double the global rate of energy-efficiency improvement from roughly 2% to about 4% per year. (A practical aside—because it lies in our hands as consumers: energy efficiency means achieving maximum output in a given activity with the least possible energy input, in short, consuming differently. This may be the other face of the energy revolution: what each of us can do.)

Yet the starting point of this transition remains striking: roughly eighty percent of global primary energy still comes from fossil fuels. At the same time, new technologies are attracting increasing attention and capital.

---

sis-wind-and-solar-added-more-to-global-energy-than-any-other-source-in-2023/ (Accessed October 27, 2025).

[5] International Renewable Energy Agency (IRENA), *Renewable Capacity Statistics 2025* (Abu Dhabi: IRENA, March 2025), available at https://www.irena.org/-/media/Files/IRENA/Agency/Publication/2025/Mar/IRENA_DAT_RE_Capacity_Statistics_2025.pdf (Accessed October 27, 2025).

[6] Chen, W., et al., "Quantifying the cost savings of global solar PV and …," Energy Policy (2025), https://www.sciencedirect.com/science/article/abs/pii/S030142152500028X (Accessed October 27, 2025).

[7] Janipour, Zahra, "Winds of change: Europe strives to shield domestic wind turbine industry as Chinese rivals breeze in," *RaboResearch*, December 4, 2024, https://www.rabobank.com/knowledge/d011459200-winds-of-change-europe-strives-to-shield-domestic-wind-turbine-industry-as-chinese-rivals-breeze-in (Accessed October 27, 2025).

[8] WindEurope, "OECD report highlights global disparity in wind energy support," February 4, 2025, https://windeurope.org/news/oecd-report-highlights-global-disparity-in-wind-energy-support (Accessed October 27, 2025).

Fusion, for example, has moved from government laboratories to attracting more than $10 billion in private investment, driven by breakthroughs that are shrinking reactor designs. Fusion seeks to replicate the process that powers the Sun, combining atomic nuclei to release vast amounts of energy without carbon emissions. The ambition is stable, clean energy at a civilizational scale.

In this transition, an obligatory question is what will happen to oil and its derivatives. Most forecasts grant oil a long life, but not the dominance it once enjoyed. It must also be remembered that oil is a nonrenewable resource dependent on new discoveries. At the end of 2023, the International Energy Agency (IEA) again raised its forecast for global oil-demand growth in 2024, though still below projected supply. The IEA estimates that oil demand will peak around 2030, then inexorably decline as the world shifts to cleaner fuels. Not all voices agree. In January 2024, OPEC projected relatively strong demand growth and even higher crude use in 2025, led by China and the Middle East. The organization—whose members' principal revenue is oil—argues that consumption will continue rising for two more decades, while the IEA foresees barely more than half a decade before the decline. In either scenario, because renewable-energy production will grow far faster than what we may still call traditional energies, the outlook will be less dramatic but no less clear: the shares of global energy generated by coal and oil will progressively fall.

This is not a new story: it happened when coal lost ground to oil. Coal did not vanish from the Earth—nor will oil—but who imagines a present, let alone a future, powered chiefly by coal? How many, in a few years, will cling to oil's primacy rather than embrace the advantages of renewables? We must grasp that this is not merely an economic shift. Decarbonization is a change in habits, mindsets, and expectations—a social, cultural, and productive transformation that will rewrite our history.

Investment Case Study: Goldwind Science & Technology (2208 HK)

Our investment style also includes investing selectively in cyclical companies when their profit margins are low and when they are close to an inflection point

Goldwind is a Chinese company listed in Shenzhen (002202.SZ) and Hong Kong (2208.HK). By 2023 it had surpassed 100 GW of cumulative installed wind capacity worldwide, with projects in more than thirty countries from Latin America to Africa and Europe. It manufactures wind turbines, provides operations and maintenance services and digital solutions for wind farms, and participates in storage and distributed-energy projects.

China has become an epicenter of the global energy transition, leading in renewable-energy investment and deployment. Wind has been one of the key vectors: in 2023 the country installed more wind capacity than the rest of the world combined. Founded in 1998 and based in Urumqi (Xinjiang), Goldwind exemplifies this transformation as one of the world's largest turbine makers.

Our investment philosophy embraces two types of companies. First, firms that are growing have excellent management, strong returns on invested capital, and sound corporate governance—we seek to invest in them when we find an attractive entry point. Second, cyclical companies. Typically, these firms experience negative or very thin margins at the bottom of the cycle. We aim to invest when margins are depressed, and a positive inflection lies ahead. These investments are generally riskier but, if well executed, can generate very high gains over relatively short periods. Many such companies sell largely commoditized products. When supply is increased by some sector players beyond demand, prices fall and all firms suffer.

The key is that—even for a growing company—if it lacks product differentiation or competitive advantages, the investment will likely disappoint unless made when margins are very low and an inflection is near. It is a common error to rely on growth alone; these firms can lose money even as they grow.

In Goldwind's case, despite extraordinary growth over the past two decades thanks to the wind-power boom, it is clearly a cyclical industry. The main reason for this is that wind turbines do not have significant differentiation, so when supply increases substantially above what is demanded, prices fall. The company has posted years with profit margins around 20% and others with negative margins. In 2023, margins were negative, and in 2024 they were under 2%.

In the first half of 2025 we initiated a position because we believe wind-turbine selling prices will recover over the next twelve months and margins will therefore improve.

What Is on the Menu?

Let us pause (the future can wait a few minutes) to review the main renewable energy sources and understand where we stand on the global energy map.

Solar energy. Solar exceeded 2,000 TWh of global generation in 2024 and became the fastest-growing source of electricity in history, outpacing coal, gas, hydro, and wind during their respective booms.[9] Utility-scale solar PV prices (electricity produced as sunlight is absorbed by photovoltaic cells, creating charge separation and current flow) fell by almost 90% between 2009 and

[9] Ember, Global Electricity Review 2025 – The Big Picture (April 2025), available at: https://ember-energy.org/latest-insights/global-electricity-review-2025/the-big-picture/(Accessed October 27, 2025).

2024.[10] Perovskite–silicon tandem cells have surpassed 30 percent efficiency in laboratory conditions, exceeding the performance of most commercial silicon panels. If scalable and durable manufacturing is achieved, their higher efficiency and potentially lower temperature production processes could reduce material use and lower the capital intensity of solar power over time. Utility-scale solar farms have grown, as has rooftop solar. The International Renewable Energy Agency (IRENA) projects annual solar-panel installation demand of USD 192 billion by 2050, compared with USD 114 billion in 2018. While solar generation remains concentrated in a relatively small group of countries, new leaders have emerged over the past decade. In 2012, most production was in developed nations; only 33 countries generated more than 20 GWh. By 2021, that number had risen to 118. China generates about 30%, followed by the United States, Japan, and India with roughly 11%, 9%, and 7%, respectively. Vietnam, Mexico, and Brazil are other emerging markets where solar has expanded in recent years.

Wind energy. Although its growth lags Solar's, wind remains the leading nonhydro renewable technology. A modern 3–5 MW wind turbine typically repays its carbon footprint in less than a year. Over a 25-year lifetime, it can avoid more than 250,000 tons of CO_2 and displace over 2 million tons of coal, enough to fill a freight train stretching more than 30 kilometers. According to the International Energy Agency (IEA), global wind power generation is projected to reach approximately 3,000 TWh in 2025.[11] This has been enabled by unprecedented capacity additions—from 650 GW in 2019 to more than 1,130 GW in 2024[12]—with further growth ahead. In a typical 250 MW wind project, the physical turbine footprint often occupies just a few percent of the total land area, allowing most of the site to remain in agricultural use. Around 85 to 95 percent of a turbine's mass, primarily steel and concrete, is already recyclable, with industry efforts underway to address blade materials. As early wind farms reach end of life, recycling recovered steel and other materials could represent billions of dollars in resource value over the coming decades, reinforcing wind power's circular economy potential. In the United States, wind produced about 453 TWh in 2024, more than

[10] Our World in Data, "Solar panel prices have fallen by around 20 % every time global capacity doubled," available at https://ourworldindata.org/data-insights/solar-panel-prices-have-fallen-by-around-20-every-time-global-capacity-doubled (Accessed October 27, 2025).

[11] International Energy Agency (IEA), "Wind," https://www.iea.org/energy-system/renewables/wind (Accessed October 27, 2025).

[12] Global Wind Energy Council (GWEC), *Global Wind Report 2025* (Brussels: GWEC, 2025), available at: https://www.gwec.net/reports/globalwindreport (Accessed October 27, 2025).

10% of national electricity, surpassing hydropower. Wind-generated electricity has grown at a compound annual rate of ≈9% over the last decade[13] and is the second-fastest-growing renewable source there. Improvements in materials and design have lengthened rotor blades, boosting output with the same input. Blades once measured ~50 m; now onshore blades are ~70 m, while offshore blades exceed 100 m—an excellent example of energy efficiency gains. At full output, a single rotation of a 15 MW offshore wind turbine can generate roughly 20–30 kWh of electricity, enough to power an average home for a day under typical consumption levels. The cost to produce 1 MWh (megawatt-hour) fell from about USD 107 in 2010 to around USD 34 in 2024. That combination—rising output and falling costs—is the engine of wind adoption. Roughly 89% of global wind capacity is concentrated in ten countries, led by China and the United States. Brazil, Turkey, and India offer further growth opportunities. Beyond investment, growth depends on wind resources and land availability and on national regulation and corporate interest. As with solar, the primary resource—the wind—is limitless.

Hydropower. Hydropower remains the principal source of large-scale renewable generation. It provides roughly 14–15% of global electricity[14] and around 47% of renewable generation.[15] Much of the current hydro fleet is aging. Close to 40% of global capacity comes from facilities more than forty years old; the average plant age is ~45 years in Europe and ~50 in North America. This raises modernization and maintenance challenges, though hydropower remains fundamental to clean power systems. Globally, hydropower generates more electricity than nuclear, though wind and solar combined have overtaken it in installed capacity. In countries such as Norway and Brazil, dams cover more than half of total electricity needs. However, hydropower is vulnerable to drought, which can limit dispatchability and cause supply interruptions. Even so, hydropower is expected to grow steadily through 2050.

Hydrogen. Hydrogen is ubiquitous in nature—present in water, plants, animals, and humans—yet its use as a fuel remains modest (hence, its growth potential is enormous). Hydrogen can be produced from fossil fuels, nuclear energy, or renewables; today, ~95% comes from natural gas and coal ("gray" hydrogen), whose production emits CO_2 and thus contributes to climate

[13] Climate Central, "A Decade of Growth for U.S. Solar and Wind (March 12, 2025)," Climate Matters, https://www.climatecentral.org/climate-matters/solar-and-wind-2025 (Accessed October 27, 2025).

[14] International Hydropower Association (IHA), "Discover Facts about Hydropower," https://www.hydropower.org/iha/discover-facts-about-hydropower (Accessed October 27, 2025).

[15] International Energy Agency (IEA), "Hydroelectricity," https://www.iea.org/energy-system/renewables/hydroelectricity (Accessed October 27, 2025).

change. Significant production of "green" hydrogen—generated sustainably from renewables without direct emissions—does not yet exist at scale, but it is key to the transition because, unlike natural gas used for space heating and power generation, it releases no CO_2 when combusted. Hydrogen contains nearly three times more energy per kilogram than gasoline, and when used in fuel cells, its only byproduct is water. Because of this high energy density by mass, it is being explored as a potential decarbonization solution for sectors that are difficult to electrify, including steelmaking, shipping, and heavy industry. As a clean alternative to natural gas (itself cleaner than coal), the hydrogen market could grow from roughly USD 230 billion in 2024 to about USD 1.657 trillion by 2050.[16] According to Bloomberg NEF, hydrogen could then meet a quarter of global energy needs and be a decisive component of the emerging energy mix.[17]

Nuclear energy. Nuclear stands out for its reliability as baseload power: plants operate on average over 90% of the time, compared with ≈25–35% for solar and wind, which depend on sun and wind availability. This consistency will be crucial because, by 2030, electricity flowing through global grids could rise by ~30%, driven by electrification of transport and industry and by the enormous energy appetite of artificial intelligence. Electrification and AI will bring unprecedented growth in power demand; data centers alone could consume more electricity than all of Japan by 2030.[18] In response, a new class of modular energy systems is emerging to serve high-intensity computing directly, including thermal storage platforms such as those being developed by Exowatt, which aim to capture solar heat, store it in industrial-scale thermal batteries, and deliver dispatchable, 24/7 power for AI data centers without relying on rare-earth-intensive supply chains. A uranium fuel pellet, about the size of a gummy bear, can produce as much energy as roughly a ton of coal, 150 gallons of oil, or 17,000 cubic feet of natural gas. Nuclear energy has a lot of potential. Currently it provides around 10% of global electricity and, per the IEA, should at least triple its capacity by 2050.[19] Its role is not to compete

[16] Astute Analytica, *Hydrogen Market – Industry Report* (Astute Analytica: [year if known]), available at https://www.astuteanalytica.com/industry-report/hydrogen-market (Accessed October 27, 2025).

[17] Bloomberg NEF (BNEF), *Hydrogen Economy Outlook – Key Messages* (London: Bloomberg Finance L.P., March 30, 2020), https://data.bloomberglp.com/professional/sites/24/BNEF-Hydrogen-Economy-Outlook-Key-Messages-30-Mar-2020.pdf (Accessed October 27, 2025).

[18] International Energy Agency (IEA), "AI is set to drive surging electricity demand from data centers while offering the potential to transform how the energy sector works," April 10, 2025, https://www.iea.org/news/ai-is-set-to-drive-surging-electricity-demand-from-data-centres-while-offering-the-potential-to-transform-how-the-energy-sector-works (Accessed October 27, 2025).

[19] U.S. Department of Energy, *"At COP28, Countries Launch Declaration to Triple Nuclear Energy Capacity by 2050, Recognizing the Key Role of Nuclear Energy in Reaching Net Zero,"* December 1, 2023. Available

but to complement—ensuring near-continuous generation, reducing fossil-fuel dependence, and enhancing grid resilience in an electrified, digital world.

The transition to renewables will create winners and losers—that is clear. It is also clear the world will need far more energy, especially if AI is to continue advancing.

Among corporate winners are leaders in solar and wind such as Iberdrola, NextEra Energy, and Enel. Producers of key inputs—panels, turbines, batteries, and green hydrogen—also benefit. Manufacturers such as Vestas in Europe and Goldwind in China lead turbine production, improving capacity factors through technological innovation and building service businesses with defensive margins. In solar, companies like LONGi, Jinko, and First Solar gain from cell-efficiency advances and long-term contracts for critical inputs. In the intelligence and storage layer, players such as Enphase, SolarEdge, CATL, and Tesla Energy capture value by making renewables competitive as dispatchable power.

At the country level, China dominates the global value chain for solar panels, batteries, and turbines thanks to scale and state support, while the European Union leads in offshore wind and in building interconnection networks.

Losers tend to be tied to high-marginal-cost fossil flows or exposed to carbon pricing. Some firms, like BP and Shell, have attempted pivots to renewables, albeit tentatively. Others, such as Aramco, continue to bet on decades of profitable oil. In any scenario, their influence will diminish relative to the green ecosystem. Countries overly dependent on hydrocarbons—Venezuela, Russia, Nigeria, and Saudi Arabia—also risk losing if they fail to diversify in time.

The Players on the Energy Map

In the nineteenth and twentieth centuries, nations secured preeminence through control of physical resources and territory. Conquest and war were common instruments of that power logic. What place—if not marginal or subordinate—could medium or small countries occupy if they were not strategically located, lacked favorable trade borders, or did not possess proven oil reserves or other prized resources?

---

at: https://www.energy.gov/articles/cop28-countries-launch-declaration-triple-nuclear-energy-capacity-2050-recognizing-key (Accessed October 27, 2025).

What role did Iceland and Norway play in the twentieth century? Now consider the years ahead: What roles will they play in the twenty-first century, having supplied nearly 100% of domestic electricity from renewables? Iceland has done so with geothermal and hydropower; Norway—with enviable oil reserves—has done so primarily with hydropower. Who, during the Cold War, would have imagined a world looking to Iceland and Norway with new eyes?

Iceland enjoys a natural advantage for renewables but also made the visionary choice to foster clean-energy development decades ago. Located in an active geothermal zone with abundant subsurface heat for electricity generation, and endowed with rivers and lakes suitable for hydropower, Iceland has coupled public support for R&D with a favorable regulatory framework, attracting investment and making it a world leader and model in renewables. Norway, for its part, is noteworthy because, though a major oil exporter, about 97% of its electricity comes from renewables, mainly hydropower.

Germany offers another, very different example. Consider the present and future of this industrial nation that so shaped the twentieth century. In 2024, roughly 59% of its electricity came from renewables, primarily wind and solar.[20] Germany's success reflects sustained policy support, including a target of 80% by 2030,[21] robust private-sector investment and innovation, and a populace environmentally aware and willing to back renewable initiatives.

The European Union as a whole is a bellwether of the transition. In 2024, the EU led the world in renewable generation, producing ≈47% of its power from renewables,[22] versus ≈38% in China[23] and ≈24% in the United States.[24] This is not new: Europe has long been at the forefront of wind and solar adoption and has set ambitious transition targets.

The United States sits at the other end of the spectrum—an influential but relatively inconsistent player, with progress uneven across states. History is rarely free of contradictions. China, the world's second-largest economy, plays a decisive role in the march to a decarbonized future: while the

[20] Global Wind Energy Council (GWEC), Global Wind Report (Brussels: GWEC, 2025), available at: https://www.gwec.net/reports/globalwindreport (Accessed October 27, 2025).

[21] International Energy Agency (IEA), "Germany," https://www.iea.org/countries/germany (Accessed October 27, 2025).

[22] Ember, European Electricity Review 2025, https://ember-energy.org/latest-insights/european-electricity-review-2025/ (Accessed October 27, 2025).

[23] Ember, China: Energy Trends, https://www.ember-energy.org/countries-and-regions/china/ (Accessed October 27, 2025).

[24] Electrek, "Renewables generated 24.2 % of US electricity in 2024 (EIA data)," February 27, 2025, https://electrek.co/2025/02/27/renewables-generated-24-percent-us-electricity-2024-eia-data/ (Accessed October 27, 2025).

leading consumer of coal, it has aggressively developed renewables and electric vehicles—the two sectors bearing both the responsibility and opportunity for emissions reductions.

Across the ocean, Costa Rica—a very small country with no armed forces and limited strategic weight—has repeatedly supplied more than 98% of its electricity from renewables.[25] Its mix of hydro, geothermal, wind, and solar demonstrates how a diversified portfolio can provide a reliable, sustainable base of generation. Latin America as a region has abundant water and is the world leader in hydroelectric generation. Countries such as Chile and Brazil, with significant water resources, have developed dams that provide low-cost, clean power with storage advantages over solar and wind.

A large hydroelectric dam can generate tens of terawatt-hours per year, equivalent to the output of tens of millions of solar panels. Many dams also serve as water reservoirs for agriculture and flood control. Studies suggest that adding floating solar to existing hydropower reservoirs could unlock several thousand terawatt-hours of additional global electricity potential, offering a land-efficient way to expand clean generation.

The prospects are revealing and promising. How would we redraw the world map if we incorporated projections for newly strategic countries and emerging markets? As renewable technologies advance and become more efficient, generation costs will fall; cheaper energy will mean higher productivity and economic growth. And because renewables are not scarce commodities, it is reasonable to value their contribution not only to decarbonization but also to a world with fewer geopolitical conflicts.

For now, agreements to advance decarbonization—and to sustain it—still dance to geopolitics' tune. The war in Ukraine, however, accelerated recognition of the need to reduce dependence on countries such as Russia—a major energy player, among the world's top three oil producers alongside Saudi Arabia and the United States. Russia is also the second-largest gas producer after the United States and holds the largest gas reserves. The European Union, long dependent on Russian gas every winter, not only defended Ukraine but also acted in self-defense by accelerating renewables to limit this high-risk factor. This is an opportunity for the region to reshape its energy situation.

In the coming decades, the shift to renewables is likely to alter the geopolitical map. The nature of renewable energy differs radically from that of fossil energy: sun and wind are not imported, traded, or conquered. The rules

[25] Climate Action Tracker, "Costa Rica – Policies & Action," https://climateactiontracker.org/countries/costa-rica/policies-action/ (Accessed October 27, 2025).

of the game change. The historical power of petrostates could be relativized. Countries unwilling to depend on Russia or the Middle East for oil and gas will accelerate renewable investment. International competition—not necessarily conflict—will tilt towards producing renewable-energy technologies (panels, batteries) and the natural resources they require (lithium, cobalt, and rare earths)—topics taken up in the chapter on the materials with which we will build the future.

In any case, renewables are here to stay, regardless of geopolitical conflicts. This raises an inevitable question: can anything be done with the surplus greenhouse gases already emitted? Yes. A growing field is carbon capture and utilization (CCU), which could enable new applications, such as synthetic fuels, chemicals, and construction aggregates derived from captured CO_2.

In the last two years, global leaders have added nuance to the conversation. Fatih Birol, Executive Director of the IEA, put it plainly: "The transition to clean energy is unstoppable. It's not a question of if, but how soon—and the sooner, the better for all of us." UN Secretary-General António Guterres struck a similarly optimistic note: "There are no price spikes for sunshine. There are no embargos on the wind… we are on the cusp of a new era. Fossil fuels are running out of road."[26] These statements reinforce not only the economic viability of renewables but also their role as foundations of energy security and global stability.

From the corporate side, Mads Nipper, CEO of Ørsted, offers an inspiring practitioner's perspective: his company moved from near-total reliance on fossil fuels in 2009 to global leadership in renewables. Nipper emphasizes that the energy transition must go hand-in-hand with ecological restoration—citing initiatives such as the BioReef project, which integrates biodiversity into the new energy economy—and warns: "We need massive investment in green energy and an end to fossil-fuel subsidies.[27]"

One effort drawing particular attention, especially in CO_2 capture, is seaweed reforestation. Nearly five years ago, a Yale University report asked: "How can we use the ocean to combat climate change?" New research suggested that underwater forests—macroalgae—offer a promising, understudied opportunity for mitigation. A 2016 *Nature Geoscience* paper by Dorte Krause-Jensen and Carlos Duarte estimated that macroalgae could sequester up to

[26] "António Guterres: climate breakthrough on clean energy and fossil fuels," The Guardian, 22 July 22, 2025, https://www.theguardian.com/environment/2025/jul/22/antonio-guterres-climate-breakthrough-clean-energy-fossil-fuels (Accessed October 27, 2025).

[27] Nipper, Mads, "TIME100 Climate 2024 – Mads Nipper," TIME, November 12, 2024, https://time.com/7172545/mads-nipper/ (Accessed October 27, 2025).

173 teragrams of carbon per year—equivalent to the annual emissions of ~134 million passenger vehicles or ~1.5 billion barrels of oil.[28]

Almost a decade on, underwater forests are a reality under active development around the globe—and not only in oceans. In 2023, UK-based Brilliant Planet made headlines by leasing more than 6,000 hectares in the Sahara Desert to cultivate algae, mimicking natural marine algal blooms in giant ponds. We will undoubtedly learn much more about such applications in the years ahead—the incremental changes that will gradually reshape our future lives.

We are learning to change, and that takes time. We ourselves are in transition; no matter how many obstacles we must overcome, this change is irreversible. In the words of Al Gore, former US Vice President and environmental pioneer:

> Do you see that pale blue dot? That's us. Everything that has happened in human history has happened on that pixel. Every triumph and every tragedy, every war, every famine, every great advance… It's our only home. And that is what's at stake—our ability to live on planet Earth, to have a future as a civilization. I believe this is a moral question. This is the time to address it. It is our time to rise and secure our future.

[28] Christensen, Ben, "Underwater Forests: A New Opportunity for Climate Change Mitigation," Yale Environment Review, March 24, 2020, https://environment-review.yale.edu/underwater-forests-new-opportunity-climate-change-mitigation (Accessed October 27, 2025).

Part II

Crossing Lives

4

The Future Has Arrived: Artificial Intelligence and Automation

The best way to predict the future is to create it.

Peter Drucker

Metropolis, 1927. *Alphaville*, 1965. *2001: A Space Odyssey*, 1968. *Silent Running*, 1972. *Star Wars*, 1977. *Blade Runner*, 1980. *WarGames*, 1983. *The Terminator*, 1984. *RoboCop*, 1987. *The Matrix*, 1999. *A.I. Artificial Intelligence*, 2001. *Resident Evil*, 2002. *I, Robot*, 2004. *WALL-E*, 2008. *Her*, 2013. *Interstellar*, 2014. *Mission: Impossible – Dead Reckoning Part One*, 2023.

It used to be science fiction. Not anymore.

There is no longer anything "literary" or fanciful about artificial intelligence—nothing an author's imagination can project beyond what scientists and engineers have been building in recent years. No film would be long or complex enough to encompass everything leading experts (Brian Christian, Kai-Fu Lee, Daron Acemoglu, and Hilke Schellmann) assert or to portray the depth and reach of the transformations AI is generating in our daily lives. Nor is that necessary: it is all happening now. Reality has overtaken fiction.

Let us begin at the beginning, because the definition is not as obvious as it seems: artificial intelligence is the "brain" of any robot or humanoid. The industry around robots and humanoids will be among the largest in the world. Humanoids will be deployed for customer service, health and caregiving, household assistance and educational tutoring, manufacturing, entertainment (even as presenters and actors), in exploration of extreme environments, and security. Robots will include autonomous cars, buses, and trucks; they will handle deliveries; they will be vacuums, cleaners, drones, and much more. Humanoid robot prototypes today cost from under $20,000 for entry-level

P. M. Danziger, *Capital (R)evolution*,
https://doi.org/10.1007/978-3-032-31602-8_4

units to several hundred thousand for advanced platforms. Industrial robotics is already a $40+ billion annual market.

The debate between more-or-less optimistic—and more-or-less pessimistic—views about the penetration of AI and automation (read: robotization) in our present and future lives has many facets. So have all advances in human history. When the telescope was created in the early seventeenth century, we were able for the first time to observe a world that extended far beyond our planet. We discovered the depths of space, learned of distant galaxies, and saw stars that had hitherto been invisible. A new, unknown, and immeasurable world opened before us. Telescopes did not leave us inert in the face of such discovery; on the contrary, they expanded our understanding of the universe we inhabit. Similarly, it lies in our hands to ensure that AI broadens our cognitive horizons and helps us do what, until now, we have been unable to do.

In *AI 2041*, Kai-Fu Lee offers a key in this regard with a simple thesis: it is humans, not machines, who stand at the vanguard of this foundational moment of our existence. Getting the dance between AI and society right would undoubtedly be the greatest achievement in human history. We are the masters of our destiny, and no technological revolution will ever change that.

A History of Intelligence

For a little over the first half of the twentieth century, the idea of intelligent machines was associated with science fiction—specifically, literary and cinematic narratives in which androids, intelligent machines, and darker variants took center stage in iconic works. In the last decades of the century, however, the theme leapt from fiction into laboratories. Scientists, engineers, mathematicians, and other technologists began trying to realize something that initially seemed a contradiction in terms: artificial intelligence.

From the mid-1980s, the spread of personal computers enabled the progressive digitization of human activities. Data were generated, stored, and manipulated with ever greater ease. At that time, by "data" we mainly meant words and simple images: as the word processor replaced the now-obsolete typewriter—a relic of not-so-distant analogue times—we began to write faster and more, to erase our mistakes and rewrite indefinitely. Our idea of limits began to shift.

In a world where the written word still reigned over the image, text creation suddenly became simpler, and for a while this amounted to a modest revolution. Then, in the 1990s, that technological ferment made a qualitative leap with the invention of the Internet. Everything began to change.

The "network of networks" completely transformed communications and access to information. Google was born in 1998, Facebook in 2004, YouTube in 2005, and WhatsApp in 2009. All of this happened in very little time. In just over a decade, legendary companies appeared that are now woven into everyday life, almost without our noticing the revolution they represented not long ago. Google revolutionized access to information, Facebook the dynamics of social interaction, and WhatsApp the way we communicate. Did anyone think this transformation would stop there? When in human history has a radical change in one industry been contained before triggering a chain reaction across other sectors of the economy and society? Why would this time be an exception, when that initial change—the original tsunami of the 1990s—was of unknown and incalculable depth?

"The world has changed more in the last hundred years than in any other century in history. The cause is not political or economic, but technological," Stephen Hawking observed. Some forces are, by their nature, unstoppable. This is such a case, and we are now living through a new turn in the technological narrative: how to make intelligent use of the vast quantities of data generated by this new way of living and relating to one another.

For in addition to "intelligence," technology has reached another faculty we long assumed was exclusively human: learning. AI and machine learning (ML) enable the analysis of enormous quantities of data and the extraction of valuable information. We are speaking of volumes the human brain could, in principle, process, but only on inhuman timescales—we would die before the results had any value or relevance. This automated processing goes far beyond mere data collection. It is not simple accumulation; this is where learning enters. Machines can increasingly *understand* data and make *predictions*; they can draw lessons from an almost infinite set of information and help make more informed, more efficient decisions in almost any field of human activity.

Machine learning rests on precisely this: the capacity of computers to analyze large datasets and find hidden patterns and relationships—nonobvious meaning, as when music is created from invisible patterns of sounds and harmonies. It is, in a sense, a mechanism that replicates the human brain—only at a far larger, nonhuman scale. Hence, we can speak of intelligence—artificial, yes, but intelligence, nonetheless. After all, whatever its nature, intelligence consists in learning from available information in order to do better whatever we do.

Let us return to basics and recall a few core Oxford English Dictionary definitions to grasp the scale of this change:

intelligence, *n.* The faculty of understanding; intellect. Also, as a count noun: a mental manifestation of this faculty; capacity for understanding.

artificial, *adj. & n.* Of a thing: made or constructed by human skill, esp. in imitation of, or as a substitute for, something made or produced naturally; man-made.

automation, *n.* The action or process of making automatic, habitual or reproducible without conscious thought a behavior, language, etc.

learn, *v.* To acquire knowledge or skill by study, experience, instruction, etc.

AI seeks to simulate and emulate these human abilities through algorithms and computational systems. This includes reasoning, learning, visual perception, linguistic interaction, and decision-making, among others. It also uses artificial neural networks—computational models inspired by the structure and functioning of our brain; like biological neurons, they can transmit signals and process information using a mathematical architecture. A Google paper titled "Attention Is All You Need" revolutionized the concept of machine learning. Now machines can *learn* the necessary rules or algorithms from data using neural networks. Consequently, today's intelligent programs are optimized for specific tasks. For example, ChatGPT is used to understand and generate text; Midjourney to generate images; and Runway to create videos. Soon there will also be artificial general intelligence serving across domains. To quote Larry Page, former CEO of Google:

> AI would be the ultimate version of Google—the ultimate search engine that would understand everything on the web. It would understand exactly what you want and give you the right thing. We're nowhere near that now. However, we can get incrementally closer, and that is basically what we work on.

Let me pause on this point. AI-driven search is transforming the traditional model of search engines such as Google: instead of lists of links, it offers direct, conversational answers that synthesize multiple sources, reducing traffic to original-content sites and altering SEO (search engine optimization) strategies. This affects news media, online advertising, and educational platforms, as new monetization modes (sponsored answers, integrated affiliates) replace classic ads. The emergence of actors such as Perplexity confirms both the user-experience gains and the reconfiguration of how information is accessed, monetized and consumed on the web.

But the transformation of AI is not only happening in software. Behind these new interfaces lies a highly concentrated physical infrastructure. Advanced chip fabrication is dominated by Taiwan, memory production by South Korea, and much of the assembly ecosystem sits in East Asia, creating a structurally concentrated hardware backbone for global AI.

In early 2026, during a conversation I had with André Esteves, founder of BTG Pactual in Brazil, he pointed to a striking reality of the AI era: NVIDIA's market capitalization now approaches that of the entire Japanese stock market, even though Japan is one of the world's five-largest economy. By 2026, the largest U.S. hyperscalers alone were expected to spend roughly $800 billion in capital expenditures, much of it directed toward AI and data-center infrastructure. Increasingly, the constraint is not only the availability of chips and memory but the ability to provide the space, power, and grid connections needed to deploy them.

Beyond its capacity to process volumes of data unmanageable for humans, AI has another virtue: it is tireless. Its learning curve improves with practice and time; it is steady and rising—like a brain that continually learns from the information we provide and that, progressively, can make ever more complex decisions by itself. For this reason, the application of AI and the automation of objects and processes cut across every sphere of economic and social life we know—and those that will emerge from our interaction with this technology, which, perhaps more than any other, remains a work in progress. The last word is far from being said.

One of the clearest manifestations of this shift is the emergence of agentic AI. Artificial intelligence is moving from being a tool to becoming a digital coworker. In certain digital workflows, one AI-augmented employee can now produce the output that previously required two or even three junior roles, compressing labor intensity by 2–3x. Rather than just speeding up tasks, AI is beginning to absorb them end-to-end, reshaping cost structures and pushing enterprise software toward usage- and outcome-based models. Agentic AI has the potential to replace many traditional software applications. As a result, software companies may need to reshape their business models.

ChatGPT: A Not-So-Shooting Star

If we consider the great industrial inventions that reshaped humanity and paved the way to modernity, one was undoubtedly the steam engine at the end of the eighteenth century. Another milestone was mass production through the assembly line in the early twentieth century. The next technological revolution arrived with computers and the automation of production toward the end of the twentieth century. Since then, the pace of innovation has accelerated dramatically. Machine learning, the Internet of Things, and now artificial intelligence are pushing technological change forward at an unprecedented speed. The collaboration between humans and intelligent machines that once seemed futuristic is rapidly becoming part of everyday life.

The most visible expression of this shift—the interface that brought generative AI to the general public—is ChatGPT. Developed by OpenAI, it is a conversational system built on large language models (LLMs), a form of artificial intelligence designed to understand and generate human language. Through natural-language interaction, systems like ChatGPT can answer questions, summarize information, translate text, write code, and assist with a wide range of cognitive tasks. In only a few years, generative AI has moved from research laboratories into daily use.

OpenAI was founded in 2015 with the ambition of developing artificial general intelligence that is "safe and beneficial" for humanity—systems capable of performing most economically valuable work at or above human levels. While today's AI remains far from that goal, its capabilities are advancing rapidly. As OpenAI co-founder Sam Altman has noted, the idea of an "AI company" may soon sound as redundant as calling a firm a "mobile company." Just as smartphones became a universal interface for software, intelligence may become a standard layer embedded in every product and service.

Technically, ChatGPT is based on the GPT (Generative Pre-trained Transformer) architecture. These models are trained on vast quantities of text, from books and articles to web pages, learning patterns in language by predicting the next word, or "token," in a sequence. Through this process the model develops the ability to generate coherent responses to new questions or prompts.

The system's growth was extraordinary. ChatGPT reached one million users in just five days and surpassed one hundred million monthly users within roughly two months, becoming one of the fastest-growing consumer applications in history. By 2026, the frontier had shifted from models that answer to models that act. Agentic systems can now execute multi-step tasks, including browsing, coding, and transacting, on a user's behalf. Because these tasks can require many times the computation of a single query, inference is becoming an increasingly important driver of demand for chips and power. Its rapid adoption revealed a powerful demand for tools capable of interacting with humans through natural language.

Behind this interface lies enormous computational scale. The Transformer architecture processes sequences of text using a mechanism known as "attention," which allows the model to capture relationships between words and ideas across long passages. Modern AI models now contain billions, or even trillions, of parameters, enabling them to perform increasingly sophisticated tasks across many domains.

If the trajectory of the past decade continues, the capabilities of AI systems could expand dramatically in the years ahead. Early automobiles were crude machines compared with today's electric vehicles, yet they marked the beginning of a transportation revolution. In much the same way, today's generative AI systems may represent only the earliest stage of a much broader transformation, one in which intelligence becomes a pervasive layer of the digital world.

An AI model can train on 13 trillion tokens, the small units of text used to process language, in about 100 days. A human reading eight hours a day would need roughly 200,000 years to consume the same volume of text. The scale gap isn't incremental. It's astronomical. At the same time, training a frontier AI model can require roughly half a million liters of freshwater to keep the underlying data centers cool.

This enormous computational scale also raises questions about energy use and infrastructure. One emerging response is the development of neuromorphic chips, which aim to move certain AI workloads from centralized data centers to low-power edge devices. Using event-driven architectures inspired by biological neurons, these chips can dramatically reduce energy consumption for specific tasks. While not a replacement for cloud-scale AI, they represent a promising path toward more energy-efficient distributed intelligence.

Yann LeCun, Chief AI Scientist at Meta, argues that the capacity to learn "world models"—internal models of how the world works—could be the key to building human-level AI and suggests a modular, configurable architecture for autonomous intelligence. In essence, this would build AI systems more like humans develop knowledge and skills over time: through accumulated experience and adaptation to varied situations. This approach could make machines more versatile and adaptable in changing environments—in short, learning as we do, from constant change.

The Disruptors

If machines are learning to learn, what happens to humans in this domain? Consider education and entertainment in the age of AI.

Platforms such as DreamBox Learning and Coursera began revolutionizing how students receive instruction and feedback years ago. AI-enabled personalization makes teaching methods more efficient and adaptive to individual needs, allowing anyone, anywhere, to access content and instructors previously beyond reach, physically and financially. Earlier experiences were largely passive, lacking adaptivity or personalized pathways. Now AI systems dynamically adjust the learning journey to individual performance, offering targeted feedback and supplementary resources.

In an extensive report on AI and education, *Forbes* noted that industry professionals are witnessing a real-time technological revolution as AI learning platforms, educational games, chatbots, virtual mentors, and organizational tools proliferate. A survey for the publication reported that although many US educators have experimented with AI tools, a very high percentage (98%) are still emphasizing ethics and transparency; the US Department of Education and UNESCO, indeed, advocate a human-centered approach. Despite concerns, US educators appear optimistic about AI's classroom potential and are already integrating tools into daily routines.

In medical imaging, AI systems have achieved high diagnostic accuracy in specific tasks, but their real strength is augmentation. Studies show that radiologists working with AI as a second reader detect more anomalies and reduce missed cases compared to either a human or an algorithm alone, reinforcing that the "Doctor + AI" model outperforms solo performance. In entertainment, AI likewise plays a decisive role in content recommendation and visual-effects creation. Companies such as Netflix and DeepArt show how AI can enhance user experience—from personalized recommendations to transforming photos into works of art. In roughly 18 months after the launch of high-level generative AI tools, users created more than 15 billion synthetic images. While global photography had already produced billions of images during the film era, AI compressed image creation into a scale and speed previously unimaginable, shifting visual production from physical capture to instant generation. Speaking of entertainment, outside Los Angeles a new industry hub is Cannes, home to the World Artificial Intelligence Cannes Festival (WAICF). In its third edition, the event produced a report on AI in media and entertainment, arguing that it is "not only a tool for consumers of entertainment to make better choices about what to watch or listen to; smart tools also help entertainment companies to improve the customer experience." The report highlights five areas of benefit:

- Enhanced search functions
- Content personalization
- Improved content creation
- Greater accessibility
- Moderation and best practices

OpenArt.ai, for example, is an AI-powered platform that enables users to generate digital artwork from text prompts, making image creation more accessible and flexible than traditional design workflows. Another emblematic case is Runway, an applied-AI company developing tools for the next era of creative production. Its platform is used by artists, filmmakers, musicians, and designers to experiment with generative video, image, and editing tools, enabling projects such as AI-generated music videos, visual effects, automated video editing, and new forms of digital art.

Ultra-Modern Times

Where "intelligent" once described people with high IQs or strong "emotional intelligence," times are changing: intelligence has arrived in objects and processes. Consider smart factories, which are redesigning the manufacturing landscape. A smart factory integrates advanced technologies such as AI, ML, IoT, and robotics. Its features include high automation—machines and robots perform many tasks once done by operators—boosting productive efficiency and predictive maintenance while reducing downtime and operating costs. Real-time data capture and analysis identify patterns, predict problems, and optimize operations. These factories will be adaptable and flexible, able to respond to demand shifts, supply-chain disruptions, and new product designs.

Equipped with advanced sensors, robots, and data-analytics systems, these are collaborative, connected, and sustainable factories—optimizing output, minimizing waste, and improving quality. Unlike the past, when production decisions relied on experience and historical data with limited real-time adaptability, AI ushers in a new era of instant line adjustments, predictive maintenance, and remote troubleshooting. Such factories are more agile and adapt quickly to demand and market conditions.

Samsung, for example, already implements smart-manufacturing technologies in its semiconductor and electronics operations, using IoT and AI, and runs a program to help SMEs adopt smart-factory solutions. Tesla's "Giga" factories (e.g., Shanghai, Berlin) integrate cutting-edge automation and robotics for EV manufacturing. Siemens Healthineers, a healthcare innovator, integrates smart-manufacturing technologies in producing next-generation medical equipment. These are early-stage examples with the potential to revolutionize manufacturing as a whole.

In January 2024, *Manufacturing Magazine* listed the top ten smart factories—Tesla, Ericsson, HP, Intel, Nokia, Siemens, Samsung, General Motors, Boeing, and BMW—based on parameters such as the following:

> A smart factory is a digitized, interconnected manufacturing facility that uses IoT, AI, automation, big-data analytics and more in its operations to ensure products are made to the highest standards using modern technologies while safeguarding employees. This enables products to flow through the supply chain and reach customers quickly.

This directly influences the future of "smart cities," true laboratories of urban innovation addressing all the challenges of communal life—from traffic lights that adjust in real time to more efficient energy systems or early responses to natural and human-caused disasters. From smart bins equipped with sensors that alert city managers when full (optimizing collection routes), to air-quality sensors across the city using AI and 5G to provide real-time pollution data (triggering action when levels rise), to water-network sensors that detect leaks and contamination: in a smart city, all these data feed central systems in real time, where AI can analyze and predict risk areas and intervene accordingly. Water systems illustrate the scale of the opportunity. In many aging networks, 20–30% of treated water is lost through leaks, costing large cities tens of millions of dollars annually. AI-powered acoustic sensors can detect underground leaks with meter-level precision, helping utilities reduce water loss and cut emergency repair costs by double-digit percentages.

Smart cities have rankings too—the IMD Business School's Smart City Index, which in 2026 studied 148 cities, placed these ten at the top: Zurich, Oslo, Geneva, London, Copenhagen, Dubai, Lausanne, Canberra, Singapore, and Abu Dhabi. This is a new world map that opens unimagined opportunities for emerging countries. Note that in 1980, 39% of the world's population lived in cities; projections suggest this will rise to 68% by 2050. The urgency of reshaping urban models to adapt infrastructure to the needs of a growing, hyper-connected population—and to the inescapable demands of sustainability—is evident.

Intelligence Is in the Air

Take a highly specialized case such as aviation: as with autonomous ground vehicles, AI will enable pilotless aircraft. This will reduce the cost of air travel and make it more accessible. Another important application is the development of adaptable flight paths: using AI, routes can be modified in real time based on weather and air-traffic variables, improving efficiency. In maintenance, AI promises to revolutionize aircraft care with personalized maintenance programs. Training will also benefit from virtual-reality simulations, enabling pilots and other professionals to train in safe, realistic environments, optimizing skills and readiness. AI will also enhance communication within the aviation industry by facilitating interaction among pilots, air-traffic controllers, and ground personnel—crucial to reducing accident risk.

In other words, integrating AI into aviation will not be limited to a single aspect; it will cover everything from design and manufacturing to flight operations and passenger experience. This is not a point improvement in one area or industry but a 360-degree revolution capable of restructuring nearly all the production and knowledge systems on which modern life rests.

In the sensitive defense and security sector, for instance, weapons systems were mostly operated manually or with basic automation lacking learning or adaptation. Today, AI enables autonomous weapons and drones capable of operating with minimal human intervention and making real-time decisions. This promises strategic improvements in three areas: decision-making, operational efficiency, and defense capabilities. First, decision-making improves thanks to AI's capacity to analyze large volumes of data from diverse sources—something humans are materially unable to do—providing real-time insights for faster, better-informed choices. Second, in operational efficiency, AI will automate repetitive tasks, allowing people to focus on strategic and analytical work, thereby improving processes and reducing workloads. Third, AI will significantly bolster defense capabilities, enhancing cybersecurity, electronic warfare, autonomous systems, and logistics management. In cybersecurity, as discussed elsewhere, AI-driven systems can detect, analyze, and respond to cyberattacks far more effectively than we can—a crucial aspect given cybercrime's global economic relevance.

In logistics, automation is transforming supply chains by optimizing routing, reducing costs, and minimizing errors. Amazon, for example, uses Kiva robots in its fulfillment centers—autonomous warehouse robots (developed by Kiva Systems, acquired by Amazon in 2012) that move goods and, with robotic arms, pick and place items, automating picking and packing. This has increased efficiency and reduced order-processing times. Autonomous warehouse robots can cut order fulfillment times to minutes in optimized facilities and enable denser layouts by reducing or eliminating forklift aisles. In some configurations, this increases storage capacity by 30–50% while accelerating throughput compared to traditional manual operations. Logistics firms also use transport systems that automatically choose the most efficient, cost-effective routes by factoring in traffic, weather, and fuel costs.

Retailers such as Walmart use AI systems to forecast product demand based on historical trends, current events, and other factors. These predictions—calculations derived from hundreds of thousands of data points—allow inventory levels to be adjusted automatically, reducing both overstock and stockouts. Looking ahead, several promising capabilities stand out. One is fully autonomous supply-chain management, moving products like pieces in a perfectly assembled puzzle from factory to doorstep without delays or failures. Previously, supply-chain planning relied heavily on historical data and trends, which were less precise for predicting future demand. Now AI systems increasingly manage them end-to-end, making real-time decisions on sourcing, production, transport, and distribution with minimal human intervention.

Another near-term capability is predictive maintenance with self-repair: AI will not only predict equipment failures but also trigger self-repair mechanisms and replace faulty parts. Self-repair—a long-standing science-fiction fantasy—is a step from reality: firms such as SAP and GE Digital already offer platforms using sensors, ML, and data analytics to improve reliability and efficiency across supply-chain equipment; Siemens and Microsoft have partnered to develop an intelligent assistant that optimizes human–machine collaboration in manufacturing. Siemens' "copilot" uses natural language to provide maintenance staff with detailed repair instructions and engineers with rapid access to simulation tools.

We could list hundreds of promising, transformative AI applications, and the result would be the same. The positive effects are evident. Our future is full of changes and opportunities, yet this does not invalidate the fear we may feel in transitioning to a new era whose definitive features we do not yet know—an era about which we have just one certainty: it will reshape everything and everyone, without exception. "Technology alone is not enough—it's technology married with the liberal arts, married with the humanities, that yields us the results that make our hearts sing." Steve Jobs

The roll-out of generative AI and automation has drawn a new map of winners and losers in global markets. As with any major disruption, the key is not to resist change but to adapt rapidly.

Winners will be the industries and firms that use AI for innovation and efficiency; those that adapt too slowly will lose out. This holds across most sectors. In the near term, winners are enablers of AI and fast adopters.

Among the clearest enablers are NVIDIA (United States), with its graphics processing units (GPUs), and TSMC (Taiwan), with its capacity to manufacture advanced chips. Their products have become the "picks and shovels" of this new AI gold rush: whatever application prevails, all depend on them. For investors, recognizing such structural positions is key: they create a moat that is not easily eroded and allow sustained returns even as technological fashions rotate. Many enablers are in Taiwan and Korea, where much of the hardware is designed or manufactured. Beyond TSMC, there are countless specialists in components that make AI possible, including firms providing power-management and cooling equipment required by AI servers (e.g., Delta Electronics) and memory chips (e.g., SK Hynix).

Another category of near-term winners are companies using AI to drive rapid innovation—especially those with proprietary, large-scale data sets.

Meta, for instance, has advanced markedly in user differentiation to make advertising far more effective. Add Microsoft, which integrated AI across its productivity suite through its alliance with OpenAI. Mercado Libre applies AI in fraud detection, logistics, and personalization across emerging markets. China offers many examples, from e-commerce companies like Alibaba, which deploy AI to serve customers and merchants with greater precision, to biotech research firms such as Innovent Bio, which leverage AI to accelerate R&D timelines.

An important clarification: while popular perception holds that AI advances have been achieved primarily in the United States, the reality is that they result from a global effort. Around 95% of all components in the electronic devices we use for AI (computers, mobiles, data centers, etc.) are produced in Asia—especially chips and memory. The case of DeepSeek shows that other countries, such as China, have advanced dramatically in AI with lower investment levels.

Rather than betting on the next visible "unicorn," it is better to identify who owns nonreplicable assets—chips, clouds, data, distribution networks—and to avoid sectors where AI already acts as a deflationary force.

In sum, winners own critical infrastructure (chips and data centers), proprietary data ecosystems (Meta, Microsoft, and Tencent), and business models capable of integrating AI to improve productivity and margins (Mercado Libre, and Sea). Losers are those trapped in sectors where AI reduces structural costs and erodes added value.

Investment Case Study: TSMC (TSM)

Companies that become great long-term investments necessarily have strong sustainable competitive advantages.

We are always searching for the champions of the next decade—the firms that multiply their value many times over. No such company exists without a clear, durable competitive advantage; hence, it is crucial to understand who can build or already possesses such an edge. This is the case with TSMC, headquartered in Hsinchu, Taiwan: it is almost the only company that can produce extremely small chips at very high yields.

AI requires ever greater computational power, all concentrated into tiny chips with zero margin for error. The scientific challenge makes going to the moon seem like a walk in the park. We are talking about almost microscopic products requiring highly advanced technology that only TSMC has managed to develop. Its greatest technical leap has been mastering extreme-ultraviolet (EUV) lithography, a technology only a handful of foundries can operate at a commercial scale. To manufacture the world's most advanced AI chips, EUV machines fire double-pulse lasers at up to 80,000 molten tin droplets per second, creating plasma that emits the extreme ultraviolet light needed to etch circuits just nanometers wide.

Factory visits and management interviews are key to understanding investee companies' advantages. Our team visited several AI-chip processing plants; it is fascinating to see EUV machines in operation—among the most complex devices in any industry. They generate light by vaporizing between 50,000 and 80,000 drops of molten tin per second (yes, per second) in an extreme-vacuum chamber, striking each drop with a double-pulse laser at precisely the right instant. Only about 5% of that energy becomes useful light.

Installing, calibrating, and maintaining EUV machines took more than a decade and required a deep partnership with ASML, the only firm that makes them. Years ago, Intel led the semiconductor industry. TSMC has since surged ahead thanks to technological advances, consolidating itself as one of the world's most strategic companies—responsible for over 60% of the global foundry market and nearly 90% of production at the leading edge (7 nm, 5 nm, and 3 nm). TSMC's competitive advantages are so great that its EBITDA margins are even slightly higher than NVIDIA's.

Companies such as NVIDIA, AMD, and Broadcom depend on TSMC chips to produce the GPUs that train and run AI models; Apple, Qualcomm, and MediaTek make the processors that define iPhone, smartphone, and AR-device performance there; Amazon, Google, and Microsoft rely on TSMC to fabricate their in-house data-center chips that support cloud and AI; even Tesla and the automotive industry require TSMC semiconductors to advance electrification and autonomous driving. From the iPhone to ChatGPT, from the cloud to EVs, today's technological innovation rests on TSMC's unique capacity to produce the densest, most efficient chips—making it critical global infrastructure.

For this reason, the company has become a strategic asset not only for technology firms but also for the national security of major powers, which view TSMC as a global strategic linchpin: the United States needs guaranteed access to maintain technological and military leadership, while China seeks to reduce a dependence that constrains its ambitions. This de facto monopoly turns Taiwan into the "silicon shield" and TSMC into the most valuable bottleneck in the digital economy—its moat impossible to replicate in the short term.

The Algorithm as Personal Shopper

Not only will industries and key productive and social processes be profoundly transformed by AI; as consumers we will also encounter a new universe of possibilities through hyper-personalized and sustainable shopping experiences. Beyond analyzing data and preferences to offer recommendations, tailored delivery programs, and proactive customer service, AI will help supply chains adopt circular-economy principles and improve sustainability—minimizing waste and maximizing resource recovery to reduce environmental impact. It will also embed social and ethical considerations into supply-chain decision-making, ensuring responsible sourcing and production, respect for human rights, and compliance with environmental standards.

As if inspired by an episode of *The Jetsons*, future homes will be connected to multiple devices—from appliances to cars—that communicate seamlessly. In smart cities, AI algorithms will analyze data instantly and enable real-time traffic management. During emergencies and natural disasters, 5G drones equipped with cameras will provide real-time analysis of affected areas, helping prioritize rescue operations and resource allocation.

Drones are clearly becoming ubiquitous. They are already transforming online shopping: placing an order and receiving it within minutes via drone delivery is no longer science fiction. Less time, lower logistics costs—this is a familiar formula. As AI continues to evolve and integrates with other emerging technologies such as blockchain, even more innovative, disruptive applications will emerge, further revolutionizing how we produce, consume, and distribute goods and services. DHL is already experimenting with drones to deliver to remote or hard-to-reach areas. These drones can transport packages without human intervention, speeding delivery and reducing costs. Companies such as Amazon are exploring drones to deliver small packages to customers' doors, drastically reducing urban delivery times. Tests are also under way for larger drones to move goods between warehouses or to remote areas—especially useful over difficult terrain or where infrastructure is poor.

Not all drones are for outdoor use (some scan warehouse shelves to ensure inventory accuracy, check stock levels, and identify misplaced items). There are concerns, of course, about airspace regulation and privacy in a world where skies are full of drones. But the future will arrive, and after a period of transition—of discovery, confusion, and uncertainty—regulations will find their way. This too is a familiar formula. Invention leads; rulemaking follows. We have seen it many times in human history.

Robots Versus Humans?

The arrival of ChatGPT marked a milestone in AI, adding risk to jobs once considered "safer." Over the next two decades, AI will automate a significant share of today's jobs—posing challenges and opportunities. Automation already raises concerns about unemployment and inequality, as those with AI skills clearly enjoy competitive advantages. Yet it is a serious mistake to infer that this will create net unemployment.

Jobs have changed drastically over history. They change; they do not vanish. If agrarian economies—communities and families—organized employment in the past, and today multinationals—and to a lesser extent SMEs—play a central role in job creation, likewise, technological development will generate new and different jobs as AI advances in automating repetitive tasks: first physical (robots and drones), then intellectual (e.g., software development), and finally, with greater difficulty, those requiring human interaction (e.g., workplace problem-solving or talent management).

By 2030, the World Economic Forum estimates a reduction of around 92 million jobs worldwide due to a shift in the division of labor between humans and machines. However, some 170 million new roles could emerge, better suited to the new division among humans, machines, and algorithms. And the amount of value created by AI is enormous. Another report, examining the potential impact of generative AI on the US labor market, concludes that AI could automate up to 30% of tasks currently performed by workers, displacing millions. Yet it also notes that AI will create new jobs and opportunities while boosting productivity.

It is plausible that by 2060 machines will be able to perform all tasks better and cheaper than humans. Most experts deem this possible, and there is no doubt AI technology is advancing rapidly and spreading into every corner of life. By 2060, human-level AI may be developed—machines able to do everything we can.

In that future scenario, an intriguing question arises: in what areas will humans outperform machines? The answer appears to be those jobs demanding social intelligence, creativity, and the ability to solve complex problems will grow. There will be increasing demand for roles contrasting with repetitive, low-skill occupations: think of an event organizer (high social intelligence) versus a dishwasher in hospitality; a fashion designer (creativity) versus a garment tailor; a surgeon (advanced perception and dexterity) versus a clinic receptionist. This is central to AI's evolution, insofar as many consider adopting a universal basic income (UBI) to mitigate the transition costs of the new productive and social model.

AI's horizon is unprecedented, but history offers perspective to size our fears about inevitable technological change. Consider a technology that now seems innocuous: the ATM. In the 1970s, when the first ATMs appeared, there was fear they would eliminate bank-branch jobs. In reality, that did not occur. In 1970, when the first ATM was introduced, there were c. 250,000 bank tellers in the United States; by 2019, there were more than 400,000. With new technologies, some jobs disappear while others are created—repeatedly, across history. People lose long-held jobs; others find work they never imagined.

Some benefit; others are disadvantaged. That is the dynamic of great social transformations. The alternative is to stand still: had early humans done so, we would never have invented the wheel or discovered fire—and we might not be here today.

As noted, the debate is polarized: optimists on one side, doomsayers ("the future is Skynet," *Terminator*) on the other. Recall Elon Musk's 2017 remark: "In my view, the greatest risk we face as a civilization is AI." Between these poles are thinkers seeking the human factor in AI—those who scratch the surface with intelligence to find nuance. Among the most interesting is Alessandro Baricco, who, in his 2018 book *The Game*, offers a simple, illuminating, and lucid idea: it no longer makes sense to think in the binary of physical vs. digital. The "physical" world interweaves with a new digital "ultra-world"; together they form a single, novel entity:

> I am not saying that the habitat of the digital hyper-human is the ultra-world of the web. The issue is more sophisticated. His habitat is a system of reality with a dual driving force, where the distinction between the real world and the virtual world becomes secondary, because both merge into a single movement that, in its entirety, generates reality. That is indeed the playing field of the new human. It is a system where the world and the ultra-world spin within each other, producing experience, in a kind of infinite and permanent creation. This is the brilliant move carried out by the web: to endow the world with two hearts that pump reality in harmony.

In a few years, the most astonishing development may be that we can interact with AIs that not only answer questions but also model complete scenarios of our reality—from public-policy design and corporate strategy to natural-disaster forecasting and predictions with unprecedented granularity. It will be like having a collective super-intelligence available to all—a kind of "global brain" operating in real time.

Imagine, for example, a government facing a collapse in its urban transport system: rather than relying solely on partial diagnostics and political negotiation, it could consult an AI that combines real-time mobility data, energy consumption, work patterns, and internal trade flows to recommend—in minutes—coordinated measures such as route adjustments, temporary subsidies, or incentives for telework that reduce social and economic impact.

The idea of AI becoming civilization's cognitive infrastructure may sound like science fiction—and that is because it will likely be the single greatest inflection point in human history.

5

Blockchain, the Future of the Internet (and of Money)

The empowerment of people is the secret of technological progress.
Eric Schmidt, former CEO of Google

It is clear that the Internet has changed our lives since the 1990s. Without HTML, there would be no Google, TikTok, Wikipedia, or YouTube today. It may feel recent, but the first web page went live in 1991. The major players of the new industry soon began to emerge: Yahoo! in 1994, eBay in 1995, and Google in 1998. That first era of the Internet, dominated by static web pages containing the information their owners considered relevant, operated much like traditional media: it was a one-way channel of communication toward the user.

The second phase of the Internet—dominated by web applications and still the one we inhabit today—represented a change in nature. Users stopped being spectators and became generators of information. At the heart of this shift was the rise of social networks. While users discovered that they could communicate and share content with people around the world, the companies that owned those applications realized that they could collect enormous amounts of data about us. They began using that data to tailor information flows to our interests. Thus was born the *social algorithm*: the capacity to influence the information we access.

These two evolutionary moments not only changed the way we used our computers first—and later, our phones—but also shattered the boundaries of the screen, transforming the way we live, work, and relate to one another. Nearly thirty years later, the Internet is beginning to change again. Blockchain technology—still somewhat abstract and at times overly technical—is giving

P. M. Danziger, *Capital (R)evolution*,
https://doi.org/10.1007/978-3-032-31602-8_5

rise to the third generation of the Internet. In this new phase, data will no longer be stored and maintained by web applications but rather on the network itself. In other words, in the Internet of the future, data will no longer be owned or controlled by anyone. There will be no way to manipulate what information we see: it will be the users themselves who manage and control it.

That is why blockchain is far more than a technology. It represents a new way of thinking about and managing what may be the most valuable product of our time: data. As American entrepreneur (and former actor) Brock Pierce has put it, in his typically idiosyncratic way: "All the smart people I admire in the world—and the ones I'm a little afraid of—understand that this is the driving force of the Fourth Industrial Revolution: the steam engine, electricity, then the microchip... blockchain and crypto are the fourth."

Although the subject will be developed in greater depth later, it is worth offering a preliminary definition of blockchain here to clarify what we are talking about:

It is not just a database but rather a set of technologies that allow the transfer of value or assets from one point to another without the intervention of third parties. Blockchain technology proposes a model in which authenticity is verified not by a single authority but by a network of nodes—computers connected to the system. No transfer of value occurs through an intermediary; rather, it happens through consensus, ensuring that the information is stored transparently at all times.

A History of Trust

Let us go far back in time. Throughout the long history of commerce, every society has needed a reliable record of its transactions and property. Around 10000 years ago, when humans still lived in small tribes, that record existed in the memory of each individual. Trust in the transparency of agreements and exchanges was guaranteed by proximity: small groups in which everyone knew one another. Because of this familiarity, a physical or objective record of transactions was unnecessary.

As communities evolved and grew in size and complexity, the record of who owed what to whom began to require more frequent updates and some form of authority capable of overseeing its accuracy. The natural step was to delegate that memory to a third party—someone or something neutral to the transaction—that could generate trust in the wider community. Whether it was a tribal leader, great banking families like the Medici during the

Renaissance, or the first national banks, societies have progressively entrusted ever larger and more centralized entities with maintaining the record of whatever they deemed valuable.

Now let us return to the present. Imagine a notebook in which every day we record our expenses and income on a separate page. Each page is a block, and the entire notebook is a chain of blocks—that is, a blockchain: a sort of digital ledger that records and stores all data reliably and accessibly.

This digital ledger operates within a network of computers. Each transaction shows the movement of a tangible asset (a product) or an intangible one (intellectual property) and is recorded as a block of data in that ledger. Each block can contain a range of details—who, what, when, where, how much, and even conditions or descriptions—and every computer on the network stores its own copy. Once complete, the block is added to the chain of all previous transactions. Each block is thus connected to both its predecessor and its successor, forming a secure sequence of data as the asset moves or changes ownership. The blocks are linked securely so that none can be altered or inserted between two existing ones without compromising the integrity of the entire chain. Once a block is added, it is extremely difficult to modify or remove it. Each additional block reinforces the verification of the previous one. Transactions are locked together in an irreversible chain—a blockchain.

Blockchain is often described as *distributed ownership* because there is no single source or owner of the data. There is no central authority, no top-down control. Anyone can contribute; anyone can read. It is a decentralized system in which no one has power over others, and each node or computer in the network holds a copy of the record. It is therefore impossible to alter transaction data maliciously without the consent of the majority of nodes. No single owner can isolate, filter, or fully block that flow of information. Everyone can know who owns the data, yet no company can hoard or monetize it. Consequently, no one can manipulate how we consume that data. This decentralization not only makes it more difficult to attack or corrupt the system; above all, it becomes a catalyst for trust. Because blockchains are distributed across many independent nodes, they are highly resistant to single points of failure such as localized outages or data center disruptions. In this digital assembly line, what is assembled is not a physical object but data—everything of value to us: money, art, property titles, classified information, medical records, and contracts. At a time when concerns over data misuse are pervasive, it bears repeating: blockchain operates through a decentralized network of nodes that ensures the security and integrity of stored information and enables transparent auditing of its records. Just as Fordism in the early twentieth century inaugurated an era of industrial production with meticulous tracking of each step in the process, blockchain provides an immutable and transparent digital record of every transaction. One subtle but illuminating point is that what circulates in a blockchain is the value itself, rather than messages instructing intermediaries to transfer that value. This is, without doubt, a paradigm shift. At first sight this seems like a trivial difference, but in fact it has profound and nonobvious consequences. The first consequence is that blockchain transactions are atomic—that is, they either occur in their entirety or not at all. There are no additional processes required to confirm the operation, since the valuable asset itself is the central entity in the transaction. This eliminates the need for settlement, clearing agents, and counterparty risk.

The emphasis bears repeating: data and information are stored on a distributed blockchain not managed by any single organization and not subject to any central authority—corporate or governmental. The goal is to create a shared, reliable information network, free of filters or censorship, accessible worldwide, and managed by the true owners of the data: the users. That is why blockchain is the future of the Internet.

Cryptocurrencies: The Most Visible Face

Throughout history, money has reinvented itself many times: livestock, precious metals, coins, banknotes, and bank transfers. Today we are witnessing a new reinvention—digital currencies created on the blockchain, such as Bitcoin and Ether—and, as before, these are generating social and political changes that extend far beyond the realm of money itself. What is truly at stake is *trust*: in whom or in what we are willing to place the custody of our value.

Cryptocurrencies were the first digital assets of value designed for the Internet that can be transferred without third-party mediation. Although the two terms are often conflated, the value of blockchain extends far beyond its initial use case as the foundation for cryptocurrencies. Cryptos are simply programs that run on blockchain technology, originally created as a response to the global financial crisis of 2008. There had been earlier attempts, all of which failed, until someone known as Satoshi Nakamoto—whom *The New Yorker* once described as a "computer coder of almost supernatural talent"—published a white paper proposing an electronic cash system similar to physical money but without the intermediaries of the traditional financial system: governments, banks, and credit-card companies.

Essentially, his paper, *A Peer-to-Peer Electronic Cash System*, explained and established the basic structure of Bitcoin. But to grasp its meaning, it is crucial to remember the context: it was a reaction to government bailouts of banks using taxpayer money. Embedded within it was an unmistakable libertarian vision that questioned the state's monopoly over the issuance of currency. Once again, this was not only about money.

From the broad view of human history, transactions conducted with currency occupy only a small fragment of time. Yet their importance lies not in longevity but in symbolism: money has long stood as the hallmark of modernity. Where currency exists, barter fades; where currency circulates, the state emerges. Since the birth of modern nation-states in the sixteenth century, they have defined themselves by two nondelegable monopolies: force and money. To challenge those monopolies was to declare war. Cryptocurrencies emerged to question this premise of modern life, offering peaceful alternatives that would have seemed unthinkable—or outright intolerable—only decades ago.

Returning to Bitcoin—the *Eve* of cryptocurrencies—the first transaction took place in 2009. Although the group behind it remains anonymous, it is believed that its members had previously attempted, unsuccessfully, to create other digital currencies. Ethereum, by contrast, has faces: it was developed by Vitalik Buterin, a Russian-born programmer and writer co-founder of *Bitcoin Magazine*, and Gavin James Wood, a British computer scientist who later co-founded other blockchain networks such as Polkadot and Kusama. Ethereum completed "The Merge" in September 2022, transitioning from proof-of-work to proof-of-stake and reducing the network's energy consumption by about 99.9 percent.

Bitcoin was the first fully decentralized, open-source, peer-to-peer digital currency in the world. It has no central issuing authority capable of altering supply, and holders can transact without intermediaries. Before Bitcoin, every online transaction required a trusted third party—PayPal, Visa, or a bank—to store customer data, safeguard assets, and process payments. These systems entail infrastructure costs and carry hacking risks. By contrast, cryptocurrency transactions, which eliminate intermediaries, are faster, cheaper—especially across borders—and decentralized. Wallet holders become their own custodians through private keys that prove ownership. Because of these features, cryptocurrencies can serve effectively both as a medium of exchange, thanks to low transaction costs, and as a store of value. They also offer (in practice and in potential) inclusion for millions of people still excluded from traditional banking systems. The global cryptocurrency market capitalization is at around US$3.9 trillion as of late 2025.

According to Mastercard CEO Michael Miebach, the SWIFT cooperative (the *Society for Worldwide Interbank Financial Telecommunication*)—still the most widely used network for transmitting cross-border fund-transfer orders—could cease to exist within five years. Although SWIFT processed more than 53 million messages per day in 2024, it struggles to remain relevant in a new international financial order that demands faster and cheaper solutions.

Even more disruptive is the fact that, for those who possess blockchain programming skills, creating a new cryptocurrency is relatively easy. What is difficult, as in any business, is achieving success—building a currency that becomes widely used and trusted. One successful example is Ripple, a digital payments platform and currency designed for rapid, low-cost transactions, especially across borders. Ripple has established partnerships with financial institutions worldwide seeking more efficient and economical solutions. Unlike other cryptocurrencies that openly challenge or bypass traditional finance, Ripple has chosen to collaborate—at least for now—with the banking system (and the banks with it, which is significant).

Many countries, including the United States, are studying the creation of their own digital currencies, or CBDCs (*Central Bank Digital Currencies*). This development appears inevitable. China and Sweden have already made significant progress in their pilot programs—digital versions of their existing currencies. At the same time, central banks are exploring regulatory frameworks to supervise cryptocurrency-related activities, aiming to ensure financial stability, consumer protection, and the prevention of money laundering and terrorism financing.

Private banks are also collaborating with fintech firms and crypto startups to improve payment efficiency, transaction settlement, and identity management. Some have begun implementing blockchain-based solutions to streamline internal operations, while others are offering crypto-related services such as secure custody and exchange.

An interesting question is whether central banks will ever allow citizens to hold accounts directly with them. That remains unlikely. However, if transactional deposits were to migrate to central banks, it would trigger dramatic changes for private institutions. In any case, the point is not whether central or private banks will disappear, but how quickly they will adapt. Their continued relevance depends on how effectively they embrace the opportunities presented by cryptocurrencies and blockchain technology.

Naturally, regulation and government policy will play a decisive role in shaping how traditional banking interacts with crypto in the future. Rules must balance innovation and growth with financial stability and consumer protection. It is even conceivable, at least in theory, that some countries might abandon their national currencies altogether—either by adopting another nation's currency or by joining a monetary union. But what if that currency were a cryptocurrency?

El Salvador, for instance, decided to accept Bitcoin as legal tender. And not only accept it but actively encourage its use. On June 24, 2021, President Nayib Bukele enacted the *Bitcoin Law*, which took effect on September 7 of that year, making El Salvador the first country in the world to adopt Bitcoin as legal tender alongside the U.S. dollar. The law also created *Chivo Wallet*, a virtual wallet for buying and selling Bitcoin without transaction fees. The government deposited the equivalent of 30 U.S. dollars in Bitcoin into each citizen's account upon downloading the app and established the *Bitcoin Trust Fund*—administered by the Development Bank of El Salvador and funded with 150 million dollars—to support the rollout. However, in January 2025, the Legislative Assembly amended the law, removing the obligation for merchants to accept Bitcoin and downgrading its status from legal tender to voluntary use, though maintaining a regulatory framework for digital currency transactions. In parallel, the government has promoted initiatives such as issuing "Volcano Bonds"—Bitcoin-tokenized sovereign bonds—to attract foreign investment and fund infrastructure projects. What is clear is that the rise of digital currencies presents regulatory and political challenges for governments: consumer protection, anti-money-laundering compliance, financial stability, and tax enforcement must all evolve alongside crypto's growth. As with most inventions, creation comes first; regulation follows.

This does not mean the problem is minor. Although illicit transactions still accounted for less than 1 percent of total on-chain crypto activity in 2025, illicit cryptocurrency addresses received at least $154 billion that year. One of the most striking cases involves North Korea. In 2019, a United Nations report revealed that the country had obtained roughly 2 billion dollars through cyberattacks targeting cryptocurrency exchanges and banks worldwide. These attacks were carried out by the infamous North Korean hacker group known as *Lazarus*, which—like everything in that nation—operates directly under the authority of Kim Jong Un. The stolen funds are believed to have financed Pyongyang's nuclear-weapons and missile-development programs. Under sweeping international sanctions since its first nuclear test in 2006, North Korea has reportedly used digital currencies to evade restrictions. Cryptocurrencies offer a relatively anonymous means of transferring funds across borders, complicating monitoring and enforcement, and regulatory gaps only heighten that risk.

These practices should decline as regulations mature, yet the challenge remains that crypto's very nature resists the constraints of the physical world.

Investment Case Study: Grupo Financiero Galicia (GGAL) and Bancolombia (CIB)

The top-down view matters.

Most investors know that making good equity investments requires thorough *bottom-up* analysis of the companies in which they invest. Yet the importance of getting the *top-down* view right is often underestimated. We believe that correctly reading the *top-down* view is also critical—especially in emerging markets.

Our *top-down* view for each country involves:

1. Understanding the macroeconomy.
2. Analyzing politics.
3. Assessing currency risk.
4. Examining the global geopolitical framework affecting the country.
5. Understanding its regulatory environment.

On the macroeconomic side, the key is to grasp the credit cycle—whether interest rates will fall, stay flat, or rise. This directly affects future revenues, earnings, and discount rates for the companies we invest in. It is also important to understand economic growth: whether the economy is decelerating or accelerating. Fiscal balance, debt levels, and the currency composition of that debt must also be examined. Finally, we pay close attention to the current-account balance and foreign direct investment flows.

In politics, analyzing presidential elections is crucial—particularly the likelihood of a change in government. We project what policies a potential new administration might adopt, who its ministers could be, and what direction they might take. Parliamentary elections matter as well, as their outcomes shape the legislative environment.

Exchange-rate movements, of course, influence investment returns. Part of the macro analysis is anticipating how the currency may appreciate or depreciate, which requires monitoring the current account and fiscal stance.

At the same time, we track which countries benefit—or suffer—from global geopolitical shifts, as this affects growth prospects and sectoral opportunities. Finally, understanding the regulatory landscape helps identify which industries may enjoy tailwinds and which may face headwinds.

Our *top-down* perspective proved decisive in investing in Grupo Financiero Galicia and Bancolombia, the largest private banks in Argentina and Colombia, respectively.

In Galicia's case, we began investing in 2013, when few were paying attention to Argentina. Politics was crucial: the government at the time had long been pursuing misguided macroeconomic policies, and domestic assets had depreciated dramatically. Galicia was trading far below book value—around 5× earnings—and at a market capitalization between 10 and 20 times smaller than comparable Latin American banks. Credit to the private sector amounted to barely 10 percent of GDP, compared with over 100 percent in China and the United States and roughly 45 percent in Brazil.

For that to change, both politics and macroeconomics needed to shift. By 2013, we saw early signs: Galicia's stock had stopped falling, valuations were extraordinarily cheap, and the public mood signaled growing desire for political change. Parliamentary elections confirmed that the ruling party could not amend the Constitution to extend its mandate, and presidential candidates for 2015 began advocating macroeconomic reform. By 2014, we were Galicia's largest shareholder after EVA, the holding company of its founding families. While we believe Galicia remains the best-managed bank in the country, politics played a decisive role in that investment.

We initiated our investment in Bancolombia in February 2025. Here again, politics was key. Latin America's political pendulum is fascinating: in recent years it had swung to the center-left—Gabriel Boric's victory in Chile, followed by the failed constitutional reform that triggered a market collapse; Alberto Fernández's win in Argentina, which also sent markets down; and similar reactions after Gustavo Petro's and Luiz Inácio Lula da Silva's victories in Colombia and Brazil. But now the pendulum is moving back toward the center-right. Javier Milei's election in Argentina in 2023 turned the country into one of the world's best-performing equity markets in 2024. We believe there is a high probability that center-right governments will win upcoming presidential elections in Chile and Colombia.

If that occurs in Colombia, the new administration is likely to pursue the long-needed fiscal reform and renew investment in oil and mining. Macroeconomic policies should improve accordingly.

Both the Galicia and Bancolombia investments, like all our holdings, are based on a multilayered process involving deep *bottom-up* business analysis and *top-down* macro assessment while aligning exposure with the world's highest-growth themes for the next five years. Although the *top-down* view varies in importance by market, it is always critical in emerging economies.

The Wallet Revolution

A striking fact reveals blockchain's economic potential: banking represents roughly one-third of all blockchain-based projects. The defining feature of *decentralized finance* (DeFi)—a set of financial applications and protocols built on blockchain technology—is the elimination of traditional intermediaries and the creation of a more open and accessible financial system in which users interact directly, without needing to trust a third party or depend on centralized servers.

This will inevitably shape a future banking landscape that bears little resemblance to the one we have known for centuries. Over time, physical bank branches and ATMs will tend to disappear, saving billions in real-estate costs. From the magnificent façades of the Bank of England to the bustle of Wall Street, from ATMs to armored trucks, all those symbols that once defined the world of money will become part of history. Consequently, the potential reach of decentralized finance is literally global: as long as an Internet connection exists, financial services can reach the world's 1.4 billion unbanked people through a simple smartphone application.

Naturally, the use of credit cards and digital wallets will continue to surge spectacularly. By 2035, it is estimated that 75 percent of the global population—more than six billion people[1]—will use digital wallets to transfer money and make e-commerce payments, versus 60% today. This transformation of how money circulates and purchases occur will inevitably trigger profound changes across the global economy.

In emerging markets, where informality is high and financial inclusion low, digital wallets—requiring no bank account—have enormous potential. They allow users to store, send, and receive cryptocurrencies through a public key (the user) and a private key. The key holder alone can authorize transactions, with no need to disclose credit history or personal data to any institution.

The same logic applies to peer-to-peer payments between individuals without banks or intermediaries. Globally, these transactions already exceed 2.8 trillion dollars a year and are projected to surpass 11 trillion dollars by the early 2030s as smartphones and digital wallets become the default interface for everyday transfers. Asia Pacific's emerging economies are expected to lead this shift in digital payments. In several markets across the region, electronic wallets have rapidly displaced cash and cards in online commerce, and within a few years they are expected to account for nearly three-quarters of all e-commerce transactions.

The advantages over cash are both obvious and profound. First, it is more convenient to pay with a phone than to carry physical money or even cards—especially for quick, contactless transactions. Second, digital purchases leave a record, providing a traceable history useful for budgeting and financial management. Third, security: biometric authentication methods such as facial or fingerprint recognition add another layer of protection beyond physical money or credit cards. This simplification is not merely administrative—it marks a transformation in how we manage value, akin to opening a door where once there was a wall.

[1] Juniper Research, "Digital Wallet Users to Exceed 5.2 Billion Globally by 2026," *Press Release*, August 3, 2022. Available at: https://www.juniperresearch.com/press/digital-wallet-users-exceed-5bn-globally-2026 (Accessed October 28, 2025).

The Other Faces of Blockchain: Tokens and Smart Contracts

Historically, the word *token* referred to an object that stood in for another of value, like casino chips symbolizing money or store gift cards redeemable for goods. On blockchain, tokens are far more versatile: they are digital assets that perform a wide variety of functions, from automating interest rates to selling real estate. Tokens can be held or traded like any cryptocurrency, but while a crypto such as Bitcoin has its own blockchain, decentralized-finance tokens usually operate atop an existing chain—most commonly Ethereum.

If the explosion of simple websites in the 1990s was followed by a wave of transformation leading to today's complex web, the near future will bring the decentralization and "tokenization" of many aspects of finance and the economy. The concept itself predates blockchain: financial-services firms have used tokenization for decades to protect customers' sensitive data, such as credit-card or Social-Security numbers, by replacing them with encrypted alphanumeric strings.

But this new tokenization brings distinct advantages befitting an entirely new system. According to *Cryptopedia*, Gemini's educational platform, the immediate gains can be summarized as follows:

- Greater liquidity: Once tokenized, assets become accessible to a broader public, increasing market liquidity and eliminating the "liquidity premium" associated with illiquid investments such as art or real estate.
- Faster, cheaper transactions: Cryptographic tokens allow investors to bypass the intermediaries that traditionally manage assets, reducing both costs and settlement times.
- Transparency: Because tokens exist on a public blockchain, users can easily trace their provenance and transaction history.

Within this universe lies the world of NFTs (*non-fungible tokens*). Most of us have seen the acronym without fully understanding it. NFTs are essentially digital certificates of authenticity that make it possible to identify a digital object as unique. They emerged as a kind of digital signature validating ownership and gave rise to an unexpected art-market boom: in 2021, a single digital image—viewable freely online—sold for 92 million USD, a record that still stands.

The NFT market now extends far beyond art, encompassing music albums, films, and even tokenized real estate investments. Investors can buy fractional ownership in a project and receive an NFT as proof. Linked smart contracts can then automate payments or returns once construction milestones are reached. Yet art remains the most visible arena: in practice, the NFT is not the artwork file itself but the record of ownership stored on the blockchain.

Why does that confer value? As art historian Miguel Ángel Cajigal Vera explains:

> If an artist associates a digital illustration with an NFT—effectively signing it digitally—that file gains a unique, public, online record identifying it as one-of-a-kind. In that sense, NFT technology replicates the two qualities that make physical art collectible: its singularity and its scarcity.[2]

While art NFTs grab headlines, proponents see real estate as the larger opportunity. The global property market, worth hundreds of trillions of dollars, is being explored for tokenization to enable fractional ownership, though adoption remains early and regulatory frameworks are still evolving.

Another emerging application, still in its early stages, is physical infrastructure. Rather than telecom companies financing towers on their own balance sheets, DePIN (Decentralized Physical Infrastructure Networks) allows thousands of individuals to deploy small antennas and earn token rewards, turning centralized infrastructure into crowd-built networks where users can also become infrastructure providers. These networks usually target localized connectivity for devices and sensors rather than full internet service. If scalable, the model could reduce deployment costs and accelerate wireless coverage.

At the heart of this expanding blockchain ecosystem lies the *ultima ratio*: smart contracts. In essence, these are computer programs that automatically execute and enforce the terms of an agreement, eliminating the need for intermediaries. They are the reason blockchain operates with such low "friction," dramatically cutting transaction costs while increasing efficiency and convenience for users. Their potential impact spans industries—from finance and trade to property registration, healthcare, logistics, and even digital voting.

[2] Penguin Libros, "Ascenso y caída de los NFT: la estrella más fugaz del arte contemporáneo," *Revista LENGUA*. Available at: https://www.penguinlibros.com/es/revista-lengua/fenomenos/ascenso-y-caida-de-los-nft (Accessed October 28, 2025).

Just as artificial intelligence helps cities detect physical inefficiencies such as water leaks, blockchain systems aim to reduce financial friction by automating reconciliation and audit trails. Globally, inefficiencies in payments, clearing, and compliance cost financial institutions tens to hundreds of billions of dollars each year, making automation a major economic opportunity. By reducing processing times and human error, and by creating transparent, verifiable digital records, smart contracts are poised to revolutionize economic life much as email transformed communication. Email automated written correspondence, making it instant, borderless, and nearly cost-free. What once required postal services and days of waiting now happens in seconds. Today, sending an email feels so natural that it can even seem old-fashioned—but at its birth, it belonged more to science fiction than to daily life.

Blockchain may appear more abstract than any of these earlier technologies—it is not a telegraph, a website, or a mobile app—but it increasingly underpins everything we do online. The global blockchain market, valued at 1.57 billion USD in 2018, is projected to surpass 163 billion by 2027 and 250 billion by 2029—a hundred-fold increase in a single decade.

We are still in a kind of digital *Far West*, a frontier without rules and with unpredictable actors. The blockchain-project bubble that swelled between 2017 and 2021—and corrected sharply in 2022, with massive token and platform collapses—recalls the dot-com bubble of the late 1990s.

Both saw speculative excess, corporate mismanagement, and weak regulation. After the crash, the Internet industry matured, leaving standing only the strongest firms—Amazon, Google, and Apple—that continue to add incalculable value to society. Similarly, since 2022, the blockchain ecosystem has entered a phase of consolidation: projects with solid financial backing, clear use cases, or institutional support endure, while regulation tightens across the United States, the European Union, and Asia.

It is a promising future—but not for every participant. While blockchain's current and potential applications challenge established industries, traditional companies can also benefit from this new technology—and many likely will. Technologies are neither threats nor panaceas; their impact depends on their usefulness. And blockchain's usefulness is so great that its most probable future is ubiquity. As adoption expands and governments and corporations recognize its potential, blockchain will underpin financial markets, enhance transparency in transactions, and automate real-estate and logistics processes through smart contracts. Central banks will continue to issue currencies—only now, digital ones—and countless startups will still emerge to disrupt and confuse.

This is the transition to a new Internet era—one that investor and Fidelity CEO Abigail Johnson celebrated succinctly:

> I love this stuff—Bitcoin, Ethereum, blockchain—and what the future holds for us.

6

The Possible Universes of the Metaverse

The empires of the future are the empires of the mind.

Winston Churchill

Do you remember what life was like before the Internet? Not LIFE in capital letters, but life itself—the hurried, everyday kind that rushes past us. We might imagine it as a sort of *matryoshka* doll filled with things that, when looked back on, seem almost unbelievable. *Matryoshkas*—or Russian nesting dolls—are hollow figures that contain smaller dolls within: there is always one more waiting to surprise us.

In the early 1970s, computers first began exchanging data. The amounts of data were tiny by today's standards, yet the point was momentous: PCs could talk to each other. Then came the World Wide Web, and suddenly a million machines were connected across the planet. Does that sound like a lot? Let's leave aside the debate over whether that is a lot or a little and look at one concrete figure: by 2025, the network counted about 5.65 billion users. Whatever the number, nothing was ever the same again.

Soon we no longer needed to queue at the post office to send a letter—email accomplished in seconds what had once taken weeks. We could search for information in an online encyclopedia, build networks of friends we might never meet "in real life," listen to all the music we wanted, and never get lost again thanks to the miraculous maps on our phones. We paid bills without standing in line, made once-unthinkable investments, bought everything imaginable, played games, googled, binged, and streamed.

P. M. Danziger, *Capital (R)evolution*,
https://doi.org/10.1007/978-3-032-31602-8_6

Each time we approached the limits of disbelief over what our PC, Mac, or friendly BlackBerry could do, something new appeared that took it all to the next level—at dizzying speed.

In just over two decades, everything changed. We adapted almost effortlessly, and there is no going back. Yet the present is not an endpoint. In fact, all these marvels that so transformed our lives are already old—perhaps soon we will call them *obsolete*. That is what this chapter is about: what comes next.

Let's see what Mark Zuckerberg, creator of one of the landmarks of the Internet revolution—Facebook—and now CEO of Meta, has to say:

> Very soon we'll reach a point where we'll be physically with some of our friends while others will be there digitally, as avatars or holograms, and they'll feel just as present as everyone else. You'll walk into a meeting and sit at a table with people who are physically there and others who are there digitally as holograms, but they'll sit at the table with you. In the future, instead of making a phone call, you'll be able to sit as a hologram on my couch—or I'll sit as a hologram on yours—and it will truly feel like we're in the same place, even if we're in different states or countries, thousands of miles apart.

Friends of My Friends Are My Friends

In a January 2023 article titled *"What Is the Metaverse, Exactly?"* Wired adopted its characteristically skeptical-avant-garde tone: "For gurus like Mark Zuckerberg or Satya Nadella, the metaverse is the future of the Internet. Or it's a video game. Or perhaps it's a deeply uncomfortable, worse version of Zoom." The magazine's brand is to question whatever is being heralded as *the next big thing*. Yet even there, the piece could not avoid listing the scenarios already under development:

Meta imagines virtual homes you can invite all your friends to. *Microsoft* envisions virtual meeting rooms for onboarding new employees or chatting with remote colleagues. Absent from that list was *Apple, which* entered the augmented-reality arena a few months later—without once uttering the word *metaverse*. Its *Vision Pro* headset is presented as a "spatial-computing" platform functioning like a Mac or iPad but with AR applications. Its key feature is a screen that can adjust to make the real world visible with apps superimposed on it.

The very term *metaverse* first appeared in Neal Stephenson's 1992 novel *Snow Crash*, which follows Hiroaki "Hiro" Protagonist—pizza delivery driver in the real world and warrior prince in the fictional one. Stephenson imagined a realm where people, as avatars, could communicate and interact. Many companies now pursue a similar idea, developing the metaverse in that direction. Early in *Snow Crash* we read:

> Hiro isn't actually here. He's in a computer-generated universe that his computer draws onto his goggles and pumps into his earphones. In the lingo, this imaginary place is known as the Metaverse. Hiro spends a lot of time in the Metaverse. [...] He approaches the Street. The Street is the Broadway of the Metaverse, its Champs-Élysées. It's the brilliantly lit boulevard that can be seen reflected, a miniature inverted version, in his goggles' lenses. It doesn't really exist, but right now millions of people are walking along it.

It sounds like a plan involving billions of people and dollars—a concrete vision of the future. The resemblance is such that Stephenson himself has had to clarify that Zuckerberg's ambitions have nothing to do with him:

> Since there seems to be some growing confusion about this: I have nothing to do with anything that Facebook is doing with respect to the Metaverse, apart from the obvious fact that they're using a term I coined in *Snow Crash*. There's been no communication between Facebook and me and no business relationship whatsoever.

Stephenson however, has become one of the metaverse's most committed builders, co-founding the blockchain project Lamina1 in 2022 to promote an open, interoperable alternative to the corporate model (a topic for another chapter).

In his insightful 2022 book *Augmented Humanity*, Argentine market-trend analyst Guillermo Oliveto picks up on Italian writer Alessandro Baricco's argument that it no longer makes sense to think in the binary logic of *physical versus digital*. For Baricco, the "world"—territorial, physical, and analog—is now intertwined with a new "ultra world"—digital and virtual—to such a degree that they are indistinguishable. Together they form one single entity: a fusion in which the virtual is also real.

In that sense, one of the most popular memes of recent years—where a mental-health professional asks a seemingly alienated young person whether "those voices" are "in the room with us right now"—takes on an entirely new meaning. Those voices *could* be real, and they might well be in the room—without being there physically.

That is what is coming. It is right around the corner, within reach. It is called the metaverse, and it operates hand-in-hand with artificial intelligence: headsets with built-in microphones and video calls, real-time language translation, image recognition, and holographic overlays merging with the physical world.

A New World, New Rules

In less than half a century, what we call the Internet has evolved from a restricted military experiment into the medium for virtually every type of inquiry or transaction, an ecosystem of information so vast and predictable that it has inspired its own share of paranoia. Yet as this evolution accelerates exponentially, one element consistently commands center stage: information—the true *holy grail* that drives technology companies to bet heavily on each new digital revolution. Today, however, we are witnessing another turning point, and the metaverse may well become its engine.

The term refers not merely to a digital platform but to a *new economy*, a *new way of life*, and a *new mode of interaction*. It represents the next step in the evolution of the Internet, and in that sense it is often described as a three-dimensional, spatially immersive network. What defines the metaverse is its integration of *presence*—the feeling of actually being there. Our lives will no longer unfold solely within the physical reality we know today.

The metaverse economy could reach high single-digit to low-teen trillions of dollars by 2030, spanning virtual commerce, digital assets, immersive work, and new health-care applications.

Etymologically, the word *metaverse* combines *meta* ("beyond") and *verse* (from *universe*), meaning literally "a universe beyond the one we know." The question, then, is how far away that "beyond" truly is. This new realm promises to transcend the laws of physics and free us from the flat confines of screens: users will interact within fully virtual worlds. How will this happen? Through virtual-reality headsets and augmented-reality devices, such as those popularized by the global success of *Pokémon GO* in 2016. Once this new phase of the online world takes off, its applications will extend far beyond gaming. These devices will become our principal gateways into *metaversal ecosystems*, with characteristics distinct from today's smartphones—three-dimensionality, natural interaction, and spatial computing. Their aim will be to link the physical and virtual worlds seamlessly.

At present, the metaverse remains in its initial development phase, focused on infrastructure building, device interconnectivity, and early industry-specific applications. But soon we will find ourselves at the intersection of multiple realities—from the creation of new physical and digital environments to the delivery of services inside them.

Digital twins allow factories and industrial systems to be simulated, stress-tested, and optimized in software before physical deployment, with models increasingly feeding real-time operational decisions. In predictive maintenance use cases, downtime reductions of 20–30 percent have been reported, and market forecasts project the digital twin sector could exceed USD 100 billion by 2030 under strong adoption scenarios.

It is already possible to imagine countless uses that will add value across sectors as diverse as real estate, healthcare, education, tourism, entertainment, advertising, social networking, and retail. In all these domains, the metaverse will serve as the meeting point between physical and virtual experience—and in some cases, it already does. For that reason, it will be essential that governments, corporations, and users work together to make this ecosystem viable. If we pause to consider the implications of this new stage, we quickly realize that rules will be needed. Global discussions and legal frameworks will have to emerge to govern new forms of work, learning, and social interaction—just as the rise of artificial intelligence, and particularly *ChatGPT*, in 2022 triggered a wave of debate about regulation.

In May 2023, the senior leadership of OpenAI, developer of *ChatGPT*, appeared before the U.S. Congress, calling for an international regulatory body to establish standards for "system inspections, safety audits, compliance verification, and restrictions on deployment and safety levels." As OpenAI's then-CEO Sam Altman stated:

> Within the next decade, it is conceivable that in most fields AI systems will exceed expert-level performance and carry out as much productive activity as today's largest corporations. In terms of potential benefits and risks, superintelligence will be more powerful than any technology humanity has previously faced. (…) If this technology goes wrong, it could go quite wrong—we want to be clear about that. We want to work with government to prevent that outcome. We believe that regulatory intervention by governments will be critical to mitigate the risks of increasingly powerful models.[1]

Toward a Contactless Humanity?

Several major companies are now competing to build metaverses of their own—Microsoft, Apple, Google, Nvidia, Epic Games, Roblox, Decentraland, and The Sandbox, among others.

The kind of socialization the metaverse will foster demands early ethical reflection from a humanistic standpoint. How will it reshape the ways we

[1]The New York Times, "OpenAI's Sam Altman Urges A.I. Regulation in Senate Hearing," 16 May 2023. Available at: https://www.nytimes.com/2023/05/16/technology/openai-altman-artificial-intelligence-regulation.html (Accessed October 28, 2025).

relate, learn, cooperate, and experience emotion? What will happen to direct human contact? Broadly speaking, social interaction will likely resemble what we already know—but mediated through immersive screens. It will feel like a three-dimensional blend of today's Facebook, Instagram, Snapchat, Twitter, and Zoom. Even emotions might be mirrored within the metaverse, though some loss of direct human connection seems inevitable—a long-standing trend throughout human history.

Anyone who has seen the dystopian series *Years and Years* will recall a particularly unsettling scene: a teenage girl tells her parents she is "trans." They respond with empathy, assuming she refers to gender identity. But the girl clarifies: "I don't want to be flesh. I'm transhuman. I'm going to become digital." If full digital conversion still belongs to science fiction, transhumanism—the integration of technology into the human body—is already real. Something as simple as a microchip implant under the skin can process payments, unlock doors, control household devices, or store vaccination records—tasks pet owners already perform for their animals with near-total ease.

This does not mean that we will soon become avatars or shed the physical body entirely. Rather, we will increasingly inhabit the realm of *role-play*: in the metaverse, we can reinvent how we present ourselves to the world. For some, virtual existence might even feel safer and less traumatic—an escape from bullying or discrimination—though this could encourage isolation and the loss of traditional social skills, or even addiction to virtuality. Such risks are not new. Excessive smartphone use has already produced issues such as sleep deprivation, poor nutrition, sedentary habits, and declining reading comprehension among young people. Still, the most probable future is not the replacement of physical reality but its complementation—a fluid interchange between the two realms depending on our needs.

The digital world presents new challenges—especially for the young—but we will never be *only* data. The future will not belong to avatars alone. Every technological leap in history has transformed our habits, sometimes radically, yet none has made us less human. Perhaps the key is not to reject the metaverse outright but to maintain a continuous critical awareness—to strike a balance between both worlds. Many aspects of our daily life, from work and income generation to leisure and relationships, will increasingly migrate to the metaverse's orbit.

In education, opportunities will expand dramatically. Virtual worlds can provide affordable, highly engaging access to learning. During the Covid-19 pandemic, education made its leap into 2D through online classes; 3D and virtual-reality tools could now enha irtual elements on the physical world nce that experience, allowing teachers to transport students to different places and eras or guide them through virtual classrooms, libraries, or gymnasiums. With only a headset and a pair of goggles, learners could explore a museum or participate in an interactive group lesson, journey inside the human body, or travel to the center of the Earth. If films are already a powerful educational resource, imagine what the metaverse could offer. Without physical borders, the connection among people worldwide will be closer than ever.

Another area of concern is mental health. The pandemic revealed how deeply isolation and confinement affect us; not everyone can endure such solitude. Equally worrying is the ease with which metaverse technologies could enable surveillance and control. Giants such as Google, Facebook, Amazon, and Apple—and their Chinese counterparts Alibaba, Tencent, and Baidu—already harvest massive amounts of user data to analyze interests and behaviors, tailor advertising, and develop products. The metaverse could take that monitoring to new levels.

In this emerging world, two groups stand out as potential winners. First, Meta, the clear frontrunner, investing far more than its rivals; and second, Asian suppliers in its hardware supply chain, highly competitive and indispensable. For example, the leading AR headset chips produced for Meta come from MediaTek in Taiwan, while specialized optical-solution providers such as Himax—and memory and battery manufacturers across Asia—also stand to benefit from the coming production wave.

Investment Case Study: Meta Platforms (META)

Growth is extremely powerful.

Meta is clearly the company that has bet most decisively on the metaverse's growth. In late 2021, Mark Zuckerberg even changed Facebook's corporate name to Meta. Since rebranding in 2021, Meta has invested more than $55 billion into Reality Labs, marking one of the largest corporate bets on a next-generation computing platform in modern technology history. Having already built the world's largest social-media empire, Meta continues to drive forward the frontier of virtual and augmented reality (VR/AR). And although the public spotlight has recently shifted toward artificial intelligence, the implementation of the metaverse continues.

In 2022, conditions were adverse: restrictive monetary policy slowed growth in the United States, and digital advertising—Meta's central revenue engine—was hit hard. The company's shares fell by more than 70 percent from their 2021 peak. Yet the rebound was equally striking. Advertising revenues stabilized as the global economy recovered and as Meta leveraged AI-driven segmentation to improve efficiency. In parallel, the company launched an aggressive efficiency program that included layoffs and cost reductions.

By 2023, the investment narrative for shareholders was clear: was Zuckerberg betting too heavily on an uncertain future or building the next great technological platform after social networks?

The investment thesis rested on three pillars:

1. A resilient core business:
   - With more than three billion monthly active users across Facebook, Instagram, and WhatsApp, Meta controls one of the world's largest digital ecosystems.
2. Operational efficiency:
   - Meta generates strong free cash flow even under macroeconomic pressure, enabling it to fund long-term projects without compromising financial stability.
3. Technological transition:
   - Its investments in virtual and augmented reality (through Oculus / Quest) position Meta as the first major player in a market that could redefine Internet consumption over the next decade.

My main reflection on Meta is this: its revenues grew at an average annual rate of 32 percent from 2012 to 2025, and its profits rose even faster. The consequence? Meta's stock price multiplied nineteen-fold during that period. The power of compounded growth is enormous. Of course, this must be accompanied by sustained cash generation, but the compounding effect of growth itself is extraordinarily powerful. If a company's valuation multiple (P/E) remains constant, any firm that grows earnings by 20 percent per year for 15 years will see its share price increase more than fifteen-fold. That is why our investment philosophy focuses on companies with strong growth potential—we seek the *champions*, the winners of the next decade, just as Meta has been in recent years.

Beyond growth, we look for firms with excellent management, high returns on invested capital, and sound corporate governance, entering them at attractive entry points. Why? Because without strong management, growth cannot be sustained. Without solid returns on invested capital, revenues may expand while profitability erodes. Achieving superior returns requires a durable competitive advantage. And without good governance, even rapid profit growth may not translate into shareholder value. Finally, our philosophy also includes cyclical companies, but it is crucial to invest when profit margins are low and near an inflection point.

Realities, in Plural

The metaverse's ultimate goal is to optimize users' digital-life experiences through virtual and augmented-reality technology. To enter this new universe, we will need specific hardware—VR and AR devices, smartphones, and computers—plus a supporting infrastructure of 5G networks, software, blockchain, Web 3.0, artificial intelligence, and digital currency. Some of these may sound abstract or distant, but in practice, we will begin using them almost without noticing. Let us briefly explore these building blocks that will enable interaction within the metaverse.

Virtual reality (VR) is a digitally created environment that provides an interactive, artificial experience through auditory and visual stimuli transmitted via an HMD (head-mounted display). On YouTube, 360-degree VR videos invite viewers to swim among sharks or ride a roller coaster through outer space—all without leaving home.

Augmented reality (AR) overlays virtual elements on the physical world to enhance our perception of it. Without being superheroes—or possessing any destructive power—we can imagine what Tony Stark sees from inside his Iron Man suit: reality annotated with data and graphics. Apple's Vision Pro headset already offer something similar.

The development of VR and AR technologies has become a race among corporate giants. Facebook acquired Oculus in 2014; Microsoft launched HoloLens 2 in 2019 (discontinued 2024); and now advances Microsoft Mesh, which enables users to collaborate in 3D virtual spaces directly from Teams, whether using a Quest headset, a laptop, or a mobile phone. These "headset-focused companies" produce some of the best AR devices on the market. Beyond entertainment, AR and VR are proving to be powerful productivity tools in manufacturing, healthcare, retail, and remote-training sectors—areas that depend on simulation, guidance, and real-time knowledge transfer.

In real estate, *home staging*—the art of preparing properties for sale—has evolved into *virtual staging*, offering realistic 3D experiences that spark an immediate sense of ownership. Studies show that over 90 percent of prospective buyers are more likely to purchase a property if its listing includes a 3D virtual tour.

Design and construction firms now use immersive platforms that let clients visualize projects before they exist, turning presentations into vivid, persuasive experiences for investors and buyers alike.

Facial recognition—already common today—will play an even larger role in future payment systems. In its own metaverse strategy, Mastercard is developing new biometric verification methods.[2] Ajay Bhalla, the company's president of Cyber & Intelligence, envisions interconnected virtual worlds where users

[2] Fortune, *"Mastercard Wants to Let Customers Use Their Faces and Hands for Payments in the Metaverse,"* May 17, 2022. Available at: https://fortune.com/2022/05/17/mastercard-facial-recognition-fingerprint-scanning-verification-metaverse (Accessed October 28, 2025).

work, play, and shop online. Customers will complete transactions simply by waving a hand before a scanner or smiling at a camera, reducing checkout times and increasing security. Mastercard's goal is a *globally interoperable system* that allows customers to access payment profiles from anywhere. Advanced biometrics will thus be essential for transaction security in the near-digital future.

In manufacturing, augmented reality has multiple uses. Technicians at Boeing already employ AR to display aircraft wiring diagrams directly within their field of view, freeing their hands, shortening task times, and boosting productivity.

Soon, 3D immersive engineering designs will interact with autonomous robots, while mechanics worldwide collaborate through VR headsets.

At Ford, engineers use VR to track human motion during assembly processes, redesigning workflows to reduce injuries and improve efficiency. As a result, workplace injuries have dropped 70 percent and ergonomic issues 90 percent.[3]

Researchers at Siemens employ a *virtual sensor* that simulates how a real sensor would behave inside an engine. AR enables operators to visualize the motor's interior with the sensor digitally superimposed, assessing performance in real time.[4]

The metaverse also promises to transform retail fashion. Instead of browsing flat images, shoppers will view garments in 3D and, through haptic gloves, even feel textures and fabrics—perhaps the missing link to perfect online clothing purchases.

Advanced haptic systems can now simulate force and resistance with increasing realism, allowing surgeons and students to feel virtual tissues and objects in training environments. Modern haptics are narrowing the gap between visual simulation and physical experience.

In education, the possibilities expand as well. Virtual-reality learning platforms now allow schools to offer interactive remote classrooms where avatars meet face-to-face. Features include customizable whiteboards, movable notes, and live video and text. The collaborative platform Spatial.io, through its *iTeacher* tool, connects secondary schools worldwide for academic projects. Students can converse directly with native speakers to learn languages and participate in cultural-exchange programs. Beyond these examples, studies

[3] designboom, "Ford's virtual-reality lab revolutionizes vehicle-design process," January 15, 2017. Available at: https://www.designboom.com/technology/ford-virtual-reality-lab-vehicle-design-01-15-2017 (Accessed October 28, 2025).

[4] Siemens AG, "Virtual sensor opens a world of efficiency for large motors," Siemens Company Stories. Available at: https://www.siemens.com/en-us/company/digital-twin/comprehensive-digital-twin-for-industry/ (Accessed October 28, 2025).

of immersive training show that participants can complete certain soft-skills modules significantly faster than in traditional classrooms while reporting higher confidence in applying what they learned.

The healthcare sector has long embraced technological innovation. In 2020, at UC Davis Children's Hospital in Sacramento, surgeons successfully separated nine-month-old conjoined twins, Abigail and Micaela Bachinskiy, joined at the head. Months of preparation included 3D-printing multiple models of the twins' fused skulls, enabling the medical team to plan and rehearse the complex operation. Surgeons also used mixed-reality headsets, which provided augmented visualization of the intertwined blood vessels—long before entering the operating room.[5]

3.0: The Age of Decentralization

The Internet itself is being re-imagined as the metaverse. The rise of Web 3.0 is transforming both the foundation and the functioning of the virtual world. Most of us still inhabit Web 2.0, the social-media web of collaboration—more dynamic than its data-repository predecessor, Web 1.0. Yet the new generation, deeply tied to personalization, is already here.

While both Web 2.0 and Web 3.0 use virtual and augmented-reality technologies, the latter enables peer-to-peer (P2P) content creation, rewarding creators directly for sales and usage rather than channeling payments through centralized app stores. Unlike the current web, Web 3.0 runs on decentralized applications (dApps) built on the blockchain, allowing participation without monetizing personal data. We often hear the phrase *"data monetization"*—it triggers an instinctive alarm, even if we don't fully grasp it. When an app is described as *free*, it usually means we are the product: the platform collects, organizes, and commercially exploits our data, with varying degrees of privacy protection. As venture capitalist Samuel Gil puts it succinctly, "Value flows far more toward creators and users—and far less to companies."

Web 3 platforms, by contrast, belong not to central authorities but to their users, who collectively develop and maintain them. The existential difference between one web and another lies in ownership and control: if an application is corporate-owned, it can sell user data; if it is community-owned, data

[5] UC Davis Health, "Rare set of conjoined twins successfully separated in 24-hour surgery at UC Davis Children's Hospital," October 29, 2020. Available at: https://health.ucdavis.edu/news/headlines/rare-set-of-conjoined-twins-successfully-separated-in-24-hour-surgery-at-uc-davis-childrens-hospital/2020/10 (Accessed October 28, 2025).

remain with the participants. A leading example is Decentraland, the first fully decentralized virtual world. Control rests with its users—those who build and inhabit it—who vote on policies governing behavior, content moderation, land management, and auctions.

This evolution has generated explosive growth in data creation, storage, transmission, and analysis, directly benefiting the semiconductor industry. Cloud-infrastructure and telecommunications firms also stand to gain, since an immersive metaverse experience will demand servers performing a hundred times more work than current gaming servers and networks handling roughly twenty-five times more traffic.

At the same time, many industries are already implementing specific applied activities. Among the vast number of variables at play, the major breakthroughs that could accelerate even greater growth in the coming years include: the development of an advanced augmented- and virtual-reality headset offering far more applications and uses for businesses and consumers; the emergence of a more integrated hardware-software platform that strengthens market penetration; and technological advances such as microLEDs and high-speed LCD displays, which improve the balance between product performance and price. All this may seem simple at first glance, but the underlying level of complexity is both deep and highly sophisticated. The metaverse comprises multiple layers—application ecosystems, development tools, and infrastructure. Game designer Jon Radoff describes it as a sequence of overlapping strata. The outermost layer is user experience, where participation is active and immersive. Next comes discovery, driven by marketing and user exploration—finding an app through need or advertising. The third layer, and perhaps the most novel, is the creator economy, marking a break from previous technologies: the metaverse will provide tools for users to build their own environments—their own metaverses. The fourth layer is spatial computing, the fusion of technologies that blur boundaries between real and virtual worlds. The fifth is decentralization, the cornerstone of Web 3, primarily concerned with data use, privacy, and ownership. According to a report by LeewayHertz, a digital-solutions firm, this layer will determine *who truly owns* each portion of the metaverse we inhabit.

"Imagine a corporation controlling the metaverse. Such a situation would create endless opportunities for that authority to analyze user activity and exploit data for its own benefit. It could shape the metaverse's functioning solely to favor advertisers and corporations by granting them access to these datasets. (…) Blockchain technology offers a revolutionary way to solve the privacy and data-protection issues that a centralized metaverse might pose.

Likewise, decentralized finance (DeFi) makes financial products available through decentralized blockchain networks."

The sixth layer is the human interface, referring to the devices we will use to navigate these environments. The seventh and final layer is infrastructure—the technological backbone enabling all the others to function.

Many firms operate within one or several of these layers: Amazon, Google, Microsoft, Meta, Adobe, Verizon, Sony, Samsung, Apple, and specialized players such as Epic Games and Cloudflare. Each technology, in turn, relies on other interdependent technologies: for example, blockchain, the core of cryptocurrency systems, depends on consensus algorithms, smart contracts, and storage platforms; game development depends on 3D modeling software and real-time graphics engines. It is, in short, another *matryoshka*: open one layer, and several more appear within—an infinite nesting of realities. A fitting image for the future of the metaverse itself.

7

Cybersecurity: How Much Will Our Data Be Worth?

Cybercrime is the greatest threat to every company in the world.
Ginni Rometty, former CEO of IBM

We know it: the digital age has changed our existence. Not so long ago, communication was limited to postal mail, fax, and landlines; information lived almost exclusively in newspapers, books, and public libraries; entertainment meant going to the movies, watching TV, or listening to the radio. Then the internet arrived, and with it came the digitization of life. Smartphones, social media, streaming, e-books, and a long chain of services and devices keep us connected twenty-four hours a day. In a word: data.

Data have become an asset for companies, governments, and even individuals—but their volume, variety, and velocity have grown so much that they have also become a magnet for another, utterly disruptive actor: cybercriminals. It's no surprise that more and more shields are being deployed against cyberattacks and that the specter of a "digital Pearl Harbor" is raised from time to time—still not arrived, but hovering credibly over every conversation on the subject.

In a life governed by technology, data have unprecedented monetary value—though not an incalculable one: according to Cybersecurity Ventures, global cybercrime costs are estimated to reach USD 12 trillion by 2030, four times the roughly USD 3 trillion they represented in 2015. It would be the largest transfer of economic wealth in history.

Where does this value lie? In data's potential to generate knowledge, insights, and strategic advantages. Essentially, firms that hold valuable information about their customers, markets, or competitors can access opportunities

P. M. Danziger, *Capital (R)evolution*,
https://doi.org/10.1007/978-3-032-31602-8_7

others cannot; likewise, with the torrents of data citizens generate daily, states can craft far more effective policies—both to assist and to surveil and control them. The same information makes them prime targets. Canonical episodes abound, such as the actions of the North Korean hacker collective known as Lazarus, which attempted to steal a billion dollars from Bangladesh's central bank, putting the SWIFT transfer network at risk.

To be clear: the digital era and cybersecurity are two sides of the same coin. As technology becomes more sophisticated and ubiquitous, so do the threats. Digital criminals constantly seek new ways to exploit vulnerabilities in computer systems in order to access confidential information, steal data, make money, or simply cause harm. For this reason, cybersecurity has become increasingly relevant for businesses and governments, even though the data economy is so large and complex that total protection is practically impossible.

Does this mean we'll have to learn to live with cyberattacks? The answer is a resounding yes. Not only because cyber risks are hard to eliminate—this is one of the fastest-evolving crimes, growing exponentially—but also because cybersecurity spending is always a step behind the threat. And although artificial intelligence and machine learning are being used to improve cyber defenses, the "bad actors" are also using these technologies to develop ever more sophisticated attacks. Nor are we dealing only with the romanticized image of a lone hacker: behind many attacks today stand groups and organizations with specific interests—and, in many cases, state sponsors.

Ben Buchanan, a former White House adviser on technology and AI, titled his book in a way that captures the moment: *The Hacker and the State: Cyber Attacks and the New Normal of Geopolitics*. He writes:

> Hacking has quickly become a powerful arrow in the quiver of statecraft. Over the past twenty years, a wide variety of nations have discovered that computer-hacking capabilities help them shape geopolitics to their liking. The result is a ferocious and near-continuous competition among government hackers; this competition is not unusual or reserved for wartime or extreme circumstances—it is every day. It has become a key part of intelligence and military operations.

In the last two years, several political and business leaders have underscored the scale of the challenge. In 2023, Anne Neuberger, the White House deputy national security adviser for cyber and emerging technologies, warned that "the line between national security and digital security has virtually disappeared," noting that a cyberattack on critical infrastructure can be as damaging as a physical attack. Cybersecurity is no longer just a technical hurdle; it is the "digital trust" required for the global economy to function. As Microsoft

President Brad Smith noted, it has become a "collective duty," the indispensable shield of our digital age.[1]

A Crime Story

Cybercrime dates back to the 1960s and 1970s. In that first stage, the motivations of computing mavericks were curiosity and technical challenge; attacks generally targeted academic institutions and firms dabbling with nascent computer systems. It was almost an intellectual feat. Yet even in those romanticized beginnings, warnings abounded: cybercrime was perceived as a real-world threat.

Born from Cold War pressures to ensure resilient military communications, ARPANET evolved from a strategic tool for U.S. technological dominance into the foundational architecture of the modern internet, simultaneously birthing both global connectivity and the first waves of cybercrime. The 1983 film *WarGames* served as a landmark cultural moment that accurately predicted the vulnerability of interconnected military systems and popularized the looming threat of cyberattacks in the public consciousness.

The rapid expansion and commercialization of the World Wide Web in the 1990s transformed the internet into a mass-market tool and, in doing so, gave rise to the first self-replicating worms, the early antivirus industry, and the need for a robust cybersecurity industry to combat rising online fraud.

The new millennium ushered in more organized, sophisticated cybercrime. Malware became more destructive, causing large financial losses to firms and governments. The 2008 Heartland Payment Systems incident exemplified the new era: hackers infiltrated a major payment processor, stealing sensitive customer data—one of the largest data breaches to date, at a time when e-commerce and online payment processing were booming—making the protection of personal and financial data unavoidable.

Over the last two decades, cybercrime has become a global threat, with new offenses like cryptocurrency theft, cyberwarfare, and cyber espionage. Edward Snowden's name perhaps best captures this mutation: in 2013, the former NSA contractor leaked classified documents proving the mass surveillance of citizens worldwide by state agencies under the umbrella

[1] Smith, Brad. "Microsoft's work to strengthen cybersecurity protection." Microsoft On the Issues. June 13, 2024. https://blogs.microsoft.com/on-the-issues/2024/06/13/microsofts-work-to-strengthen-cybersecurity-protection/ (Accessed January 24, 2026).

of counterterrorism. The revelations reverberated globally, from debates on digital privacy to policy changes in several countries. In the post-9/11 world, the threat no longer targeted only economically valuable data but also strategic and security-related information. This moved beyond individual crimes or corporate targets to include organized groups—and states. The emerging reality transformed the global map of cybercrime and ushered in a new phenomenon: cyberwars, able to redefine the geopolitics of the digital world.

Compared with physical wars, these conflicts have notable differences: they can escalate very quickly, at far lower cost, with unpredictable consequences for domestic security and global stability. "From the Cold War to the Code War," as techno-thriller author Thomas Waite put it. A salient example was 2017's WannaCry attack,[2] which spotlighted a critical issue for cybersecurity: the vulnerability of essential systems.

WannaCry—a form of ransomware—crippled access to more than 200,000 computers in 150 countries, including UK hospitals, Telefónica, FedEx, and Russia's interior ministry. The attackers demanded payment in exchange for a decryption key, but the most alarming aspect was the speed of spread through a Windows vulnerability. Damage estimates ran to about USD 4 billion.

From 2020 onward, as more people and activities moved online during the Covid-19 pandemic, cyberattacks surged, targeting remote-work networks and health-care systems. In 2021, a landmark attack hit one of the United States' most important pipelines, exposing critical infrastructure vulnerabilities: on May 7, Colonial Pipeline—transporting gasoline, diesel, and jet fuel from Texas to New York—was attacked by the DarkSide group. Systems were locked, and a bitcoin ransom was demanded. The company shut the pipeline temporarily, which supplies nearly half the East Coast's fuel. Shortages produced long lines at gas stations, higher prices, and business disruptions—tangible real-economy impacts. As then-Senator Ben Sasse told *Politico*: "There's much we still don't know about how this happened, but two things are clear: this play will be run again, and we are not adequately prepared."

In 2024 and 2025, some of the costliest recent attacks underscored the economic magnitude of digital risk. In the U.S., ransomware against Change Health-care paralyzed medical payments for weeks, causing UnitedHealth

[2] Cloudflare, "What was the WannaCry ransomware attack?," May 12, 2017. Available at: https://www.cloudflare.com/es-es/learning/security/ransomware/wannacry-ransomware (Accessed October 28, 2025).

total costs of roughly USD 3 billion, alongside an estimated USD 22 million ransom payment. In February 2024, Cencora (formerly AmerisourceBergen) was reportedly targeted by the ransomware group Dark Angels and is believed to have paid about 75 million dollars, among the largest publicly reported ransomware payments.

The Geopolitics of Cyberspace

What does this history teach us? That the wars of the future may differ radically from those we've known. Instead of massed armies or the crushing air wars of the late twentieth century, tomorrow's conflicts may be cyber-conflicts, with the digital realm as the battlefield. The object of struggle will differ, too: not land, political hegemony, or natural resources, but data—the most coveted commodity of the twenty-first century.

Cyberwarfare is also far cheaper than traditional war. It doesn't require powerful armies or expensive weapons. A well-organized hacker group can launch a devastating attack on a country that, by traditional measures of power, should have every advantage. This means that states that could never afford a conventional war—North Korea, for example—could participate very actively in cyberwar and win more than a few battles against real-world powers.

Major world powers actively compete in cyberspace, utilizing cyber espionage and disinformation campaigns as primary strategic tools to collect intelligence, influence foreign elections, and destabilize geopolitical rivals.

The Russian-linked group APT28/Fancy Bear allegedly influenced the 2016 U.S. election by hacking the DNC and the Clinton campaign to steal and leak confidential documents.

Russia had already been accused of large-scale cyber operations to interfere in other countries' politics and undermine regional stability. In April–May 2007, coordinated attacks on Estonia's government, banks, media, and other institutions temporarily paralyzed online services and disrupted the country's digital infrastructure.[3]

North Korea allegedly employs diverse cyber tactics to steal intelligence and hard currency from banks, crypto firms, and governments via state-sponsored groups like Lazarus, Kimsuky, and APT37.

[3] BBC News, "Estonia hit by cyber attacks," May 2007, available at: http://news.bbc.co.uk/2/hi/europe/6665145.stm (Accessed October 28, 2025).

The U.S. and China engage in persistent cyber conflict over technological supremacy, exemplified by the massive Office of Personnel Management (OPM) data breach and warnings from the FBI that China targets civilian infrastructure to destabilize American society.

Another paradigmatic case: Stuxnet's 2010 attack on Iran's nuclear program. Stuxnet was a specialized worm designed to damage centrifuges used for uranium enrichment. Believed to have been developed by the United States and Israel, it did not aim to steal data or sow general chaos but to physically damage industrial machines controlled by software. It was considered a cyberweapon and a milestone—one of the first known cyberattacks designed to affect the physical world.

Several G7 nations have strengthened their cyber resilience strategies by creating secure, offline backups of critical government data and investing in hardened data infrastructure to protect against large-scale cyberattacks.

Defending against cyberwarfare is as different as the attacks themselves. It's not about standing armies and territorial borders but about protecting the broad networks underpinning our complex lives: IT systems and critical infrastructure—power and financial networks, transportation systems, and energy facilities. Testifying before Congress, former FBI director Christopher Wray pointed to that specific target: "They're preparing to devastate or degrade the civilian critical infrastructure that keeps us safe and prosperous, lying in wait for the right moment to strike, sow chaos, and cause real-world harm."[4]

Cyberattacks on critical infrastructure like energy or chemical sectors can trigger catastrophic real-world consequences, ranging from widespread blackouts and service failures to severe environmental disasters.

The intersection of cybersecurity and geopolitics creates a fundamental power struggle between governments, who rely on private firms to protect national infrastructure, and the firms themselves, who must safeguard their independence to remain credible global actors. This tension forces a delicate balance: while public-private collaboration is essential for national security, firms must resist government overreach to ensure their tools are used for defense rather than violating civil liberties or becoming instruments of state espionage.

[4] Christopher Wray, "Director Wray's Opening Statement to the House Select Committee on the Strategic Competition Between the United States and the Chinese Communist Party," FBI.gov, January 31, 2024, https://www.fbi.gov/news/speeches-and-testimony/director-wrays-opening-statement-to-the-house-select-committee-on-the-chinese-communist-party

Investment Case Study: CrowdStrike (CRWD)

We use Porter analysis to identify great businesses.

CrowdStrike (ticker: CRWD) is one of the world's most important cybersecurity companies. Founded in 2011 and listed on Nasdaq since 2019, it pioneered the shift from on-premises security to a 100% cloud-based platform. Its flagship product, Falcon, protects millions of endpoints and servers in real time. Through its AI engine, Threat Graph, it analyzes more than two trillion security events per week, continuously learning and improving detection.

CrowdStrike promotes its "1-10-60" benchmark: 1 minute to detect a threat, 10 minutes to investigate, and 60 minutes to remediate, positioning this speed as a key competitive advantage in endpoint security.

Each new customer and each new event add data that make the system smarter, creating a self-reinforcing network effect. In practice, CrowdStrike becomes more efficient the bigger it gets—a phenomenon akin to digital ecosystems such as Facebook, Amazon, or Mercado Libre, where every new user generates more information and activity for the system to learn, optimize, and deliver ever more precise, effective service.

In our bottom-up analysis, we use Porter's framework to assess competitive advantages and business quality. For CrowdStrike, the moat is clear. The threat of new entrants is low: building a global threat-intelligence base and training AI models at that scale takes years and enormous investment.

Customer bargaining power is limited because switching is costly, complex, and risky. It means losing integration across modules (threat detection, cloud security, identity protection, exposure analytics), global threat visibility, and immediate response capability—akin to changing the operating system across thousands of devices and retraining staff.

Competitive rivalry exists—mainly with Microsoft and Palo Alto Networks—but no rival offers as integrated an ecosystem across endpoints, cloud workloads, identity, and AI analytics. While CrowdStrike depends on hyperscalers like AWS and Azure to host and process critical data, it maintains long-term contracts and strategic relationships, and its multi-cloud architecture allows workload migration if needed, reducing dependency risk. Substitutes are practically nonexistent: cybersecurity has become an essential, recurring need.

In short, CrowdStrike has built a technology- and data-driven moat that is hard to replicate, with SaaS scalability that allows revenue growth without costs rising in the same proportion.

Regarding how to value companies, each type of business has its own appropriate methodology or metric. It is important to understand which methodology applies and to use it properly.

However, for us, it is equally critical to evaluate companies using different methodologies, which generally provide diverse perspectives. This includes assessing companies through various multiples and comparing them with peers and their own historical performance; estimating the total addressable market and applying discounted cash flow methods; or using asset- and liability-based approaches—for example, determining how much cash could be generated in a liquidation scenario or, in a real estate company, estimating the value of unsold buildings or calculating the replacement cost of all a manufacturer's plants. Even something simpler—such as comparing the value of one company to another by assessing the relative strength of their brands, or comparing two very similar firms in different countries, taking into account each country's population, GDP, and the firms' respective market shares, as well as comparing a company's current valuation to its own historical levels—can yield valuable insight. That said, the key is to simplify. Reducing something very complex to something simple requires great depth and experience—and the same holds true when measuring the value of a company.

CrowdStrike is a fast-growing company with huge potential; accordingly, its EBITDA and earnings multiples are well above market averages. It should be benchmarked against peers with similar growth, cash generation, margins, and risk. It is also crucial to understand TAM and what multiples might be reasonable in a more mature market. And always mind the next twelve months: with high-growth, high-multiple names, any disappointment can trigger sharp downsides.

The Price of Security

Digitization has moved from science fiction notion to palpable reality, spawning new industries of every kind. Cybercrime, of all things, is the most prosperous. In recent years, attack frequency has reached astonishing levels: one incident is reported every 39 seconds (more than 2,200 per day),[5] though some estimates—like Microsoft's—put the figure as high as 600 million attacks daily worldwide.[6] This confirms we face a massive, constant, global threat. Phishing (impersonation scams to harvest credentials, card numbers, or bank data), along with data breaches, ransomware nonpayment/nondelivery, and extortion, remains the main attack vector. Various sources report that 40–90% of incidents start with phishing, and a large majority—up to 95%, according to some studies—originate in fraudulent emails or links. Broader social-engineering techniques may be involved in up to 90% of cases.[7] Despite advances in AI-driven defenses, industry reports consistently show that a majority of cybersecurity breaches still involve a human element, whether through social engineering, credential misuse, or administrative error.

[5] DemandSage, "83 Cybersecurity Statistics (2025): Worldwide Data & Trends," n.d. Available at: https://www.demandsage.com/cybersecurity-statistics (Accessed October 28, 2025).

[6] MoneyWeek, "Cybersecurity stocks: why now might be the time to buy," July 8, 2025. Available at: https://moneyweek.com/investments/tech-stocks/buy-cybersecurity-stocks (Accessed October 28, 2025).

[7] Financial Times, "AI-generated phishing scams target corporate executives," January 1, 2025. Available at: https://www.ft.com/content/d60fb4fb-cb85-4df7-b246-ec3d08260e6f (Accessed October 28, 2025).

Like nearly every activity today, cybercrime is evolving rapidly with AI, machine learning, and blockchain—driving growing investment in cybersecurity infrastructure worldwide. It helps explain why the global cyber-insurance market is projected to grow from USD 12 billion in 2022 to USD 33 billion in 2027.[8]

Major data breaches, such as the 2017 Equifax vulnerability affecting 150 million people and the 2016 Uber incident involving 57 million users, demonstrate how security failures result in massive regulatory fines, up to $700 million and $148 million, respectively, alongside irreparable reputational damage.

Insurance plays an increasingly important role because organizations must absorb many costs after a breach. Direct costs include investigating vulnerabilities, implementing security improvements to prevent recurrence, and legal fees to handle customer claims. This helps explain why global cybersecurity revenues are estimated to reach USD 262 billion by 2030[9]—an astronomical rise from roughly USD 83 billion in 2016.

Microsoft and the University of Washington have demonstrated in laboratory experiments that digital data can be encoded in synthetic DNA, an extremely dense and potentially long-lasting storage medium. Although still in early development, DNA storage holds extraordinary promise: a single gram of DNA could theoretically store hundreds of petabytes of data, compressing the world's digital archives into a tiny physical footprint.

Securing the Future

All this can be summed up in one maxim: cybersecurity will be a top priority—and activity—for companies, governments, and individuals over the next decade, defined to a large degree by the use of AI and machine learning to detect and prevent attacks. These tools will allow real-time adjustment of defenses, making them more responsive to new threats that will emerge at speeds we can scarcely imagine today, and could help personalize security according to each person's internet use. But the future is not thornless.

[8] Munich Re, "Cyber Insurance: Risks and Trends 2023," Available at: https://www.munichre.com/landingpage/en/cyber-insurance-risks-and-trends-2023.html (Accessed October 28, 2025).

[9] Statista, "Cybersecurity – Worldwide Forecast," Available at: https://www.statista.com/outlook/tmo/cybersecurity/worldwide (Accessed October 28, 2025).

Optimism and concern are evenly matched—AI will also fuel innovation in cybercrime, and machine-learning models can be trained for illicit or deceptive ends. We are only at the dawn of this new world. Governments and companies will have to find ways to ensure that AI-based systems and other technologies operate safely and ethically—and the path forward is not yet clear.[10] By 2026, generative AI systems are capable of cloning a human voice from only a few seconds of audio, enabling highly convincing voice phishing attacks. These AI-driven impersonation scams have led to major corporate fraud cases, including incidents where executives were tricked into authorizing large financial transfers.

Quantum computing poses another challenge to traditional ways of protecting information. As Amazon Web Services defines it, "quantum computing is a multidisciplinary field combining computer science, physics, and mathematics, using quantum mechanics to solve complex problems faster than classical computers." Though still developing and not yet capable of large-scale practical tasks, it is expected to "solve problems that even today's most powerful supercomputers cannot." Quantum algorithms could break current encryption protocols, endangering digital security and privacy. Hackers could use quantum methods to crack widely used algorithms. Yet cybersecurity experts are developing post-quantum cryptography—new algorithms based on different mathematical principles—expected to be immune to such attacks. While the threat of a "cryptographically relevant" quantum computer may seem years away, the battle has already begun through a tactic known as "Harvest Now, Decrypt Later" (HNDL). Adversaries are currently intercepting and archiving massive amounts of encrypted data, military secrets, financial records, and medical histories, with the intent to unlock them the moment quantum technology matures. This silent war has ignited a massive shift in the global economy. The market for Post-Quantum Cryptography (PQC) is projected to explode from $1.68 billion in 2025 to nearly $30 billion by 2034, representing a fundamental rebuilding of the internet's security architecture.[11]

With the Internet of Things, risks will grow as device counts explode: from 15 billion connected devices in 2015 to an estimated 30–40 billion by 2030.

---

[10] World Economic Forum, "7 Trends That Could Shape the Future of Cybersecurity in 2030," March 7, 2023. Available at: https://www.weforum.org/stories/2023/03/trends-for-future-of-cybersecurity/ (Accessed October 28, 2025).

[11] Precedence Research. "Post Quantum Cryptography Market Size to Hit USD 29.95 Bn by 2034." January 2026. https://www.precedenceresearch.com/post-quantum-cryptography-market (Accessed January 24, 2026).

To protect them, more advanced "zero-trust" models will be adopted, in which access to sensitive information is tightly controlled and continuously monitored. The premise: trust nothing by default—not even from inside a corporate network.

Moreover, while 5G provides faster and more reliable connections, its ability to support millions of devices simultaneously creates a much larger target for sophisticated cyberattacks, especially since many connected IoT devices lack the built-in security to defend themselves.

Conversely, blockchain offers clear advantages due to its decentralized nature, making compromise far more difficult. It will gain popularity in applications requiring high levels of security—especially in finance, healthcare, and government—where data-breach risks can have grave, sometimes unpredictable consequences.

Blockchain will also change digital-identity management. Authentication and authorization have long been points of vulnerability; blockchain can give users more control and mitigate the risks of centralized databases. This does not mean that integrating blockchain into cybersecurity is challenge-free—from the prerequisites for widespread adoption to balancing transparency and security with privacy (given that the anonymity of some blockchain transactions may pose regulatory risks). Still, the intersection between the two will be one of the most fertile grounds for innovation in the years ahead.

A related breakthrough in modern cryptography is the concept of zero-knowledge proofs. This technique allows a user to prove that a statement is true, such as meeting an identity or credit requirement, without revealing the underlying private data. In cybersecurity, it offers a powerful way to authenticate users or verify credentials while keeping sensitive information private.

Cybersecurity will also significantly affect national-security considerations. Governments are already taking steps to protect critical infrastructure from cyberattacks—one example is the growing use of zero-trust models. Unlike traditional security, which assumes everything inside the network is trustworthy, zero-trust continuously verifies every user and device, regardless of location—reducing unauthorized access and helping prevent attacks. Governments are also investing in R&D to keep pace with emerging threats, including new encryption algorithms and quantum techniques to crack complex codes. At the same time, the geopolitical dimension of cybersecurity is becoming increasingly visible. By 2026, internet fragmentation is growing more pronounced as countries such as China, Russia, and Iran increasingly control access and develop national intranets or shutdown mechanisms, sometimes restricting connectivity with the global web during crises.

A significant obstacle looms: recruiting and retaining cybersecurity talent.[12] As the threat landscape evolves, demand rises for highly technical profiles able to respond to attacks and manage security effectively in sectors like energy—profiles not easily found in today's labor markets—and for professionals who understand the interaction between technology and people. Closing this skills gap will not be easy; it will likely require tighter collaboration between the private sector, educational institutions, and governments.

We thus return to one of the most relevant actors in the future of cybersecurity: governments—and the redefinition of boundaries with private corporations regarding personal-data handling, the political power of tech companies, and the potential restructuring of global institutions to reflect a reality in which security challenges extend beyond conventional military conflicts to include cybersecurity, data privacy, information manipulation, and other emerging digital risks.

This raises profound questions of legitimacy and representation. Should private companies—whose commercial interests may conflict with the goals of the international community—have a role in decision-making on global security? How can we balance the need to leverage their expertise and resources with the responsibility to ensure transparency, accountability, and respect for human rights? How do we ensure these organizations do not abuse their power or prioritize their interests over the common good? What oversight mechanisms could ensure decisions serve international peace and security?

From the techno-pessimist corner, economist Yanis Varoufakis offers a hypothesis supported by observable facts: today's computing giants are redrawing the geopolitical map, with companies sometimes more powerful than the countries that birthed them. Varoufakis writes:

> This new mutant capital can be called "cloud capital." It does not live in the clouds, of course, but on Earth; it resides in networked equipment, server farms, cell towers, programs, AI-based algorithms, and at the bottom of our oceans, where countless kilometers of fiber-optic cables stretch.

[12] Center for Long-Term Cybersecurity (UC Berkeley), "Seven trends that could shape the 'official future' of cybersecurity in 2030," March 2023. Available at: https://cltc.berkeley.edu/publication/seven-trends-cybersecurity-2030 (Accessed October 28, 2025).

He describes an increasingly digital, globalized world in which Big Tech will continue to gain influence over national economies, societies, and politics in the absence of a robust regulatory framework. In this dynamic of ongoing tension and collaboration between two great actors—the public sector, a major purchaser and investor in technology capable of shaping how cybersecurity evolves, and tech companies, which will hold vast troves of data, critical digital infrastructure, and innovative technologies—the face of tomorrow's society will, to a large extent, be decided.

Part III

Sapiens 3.0

8

The Search for the Holy Grail, or the Revolution in Health

It is not the strongest of the species that survives, nor the most intelligent, but the one most responsive to change.

Charles Darwin

A seven-hundred-year-old Templar knight—thin and weary inside his silver armor (yet alive and well!)—greets the man he believes to be his successor: a young figure wearing a brown hat, leather jacket, and whip, part nineteenth-century explorer, part Far West cowboy, and part Ivy League professor. Yet this man has not crossed half the planet or escaped certain death a dozen times to inherit the mission of that eternal guardian. Indiana Jones is there only to save his father, wounded by a Nazi bullet, from a group of scientists obsessed with finding an antidote to the one thing that remains irreversible for humankind: death.

The Templars have fascinated historians, archaeologists, and readers hungry for adventure for centuries. Founded in Jerusalem in the twelfth century to protect pilgrims traveling to the Holy Land, the order became a powerful force across medieval Europe, enjoying papal privileges, tax exemptions, and generous donations. Legend holds that under this almost unrestricted power and legendary status, the Templars became guardians of the Holy Grail—the cup from which Jesus drank at the Last Supper and which later contained his blood. That story inspired iconic narratives, from *Indiana Jones and the Last Crusade* to Dan Brown's *The Da Vinci Code*, yet the timeless allure of that humble vessel goes far beyond its keepers. The Holy Grail carries with it the promise of realizing humanity's oldest dream: the ability to cure all disease and survive any accident—the conquest of eternal life.

P. M. Danziger, *Capital (R)evolution*,
https://doi.org/10.1007/978-3-032-31602-8_8

Long Live Life

Dreams of eternity made sense in a world where life expectancy was very low. We tend to long for what we do not have. But today we live significantly longer than a century ago. Global life expectancy now exceeds seventy years—twice what it was one hundred years ago—and this trend will only deepen in the decades ahead. A single data point captures the change: in 2003, global average life expectancy was 66.5 years; by 2024, it had risen to 73.3 years, an increase of 6.8 years, or roughly ten percent, in just two decades. We have already found our modest Holy Grail. Epigenetic diagnostics are already commercially available and allow biological aging to be estimated through DNA methylation patterns, while epigenetic reprogramming therapies are in early research and initial human trials under regulatory scrutiny. The broader longevity sector is attracting significant investment, though long-term market projections remain highly speculative.

By the mid-2020s, the world has about 600,000 centenarians, less than 0.01 percent of the global population, but their numbers are expected to rise rapidly by 2050 due to aging demographics and medical advances. The increase in life expectancy is one of the most remarkable achievements of our time. Many factors explain it, but medicine and healthcare advances certainly top the list—from the development of vaccines, drugs, and treatments that have reduced once-fatal diseases to improvements in nutrition and diet and universal access to clean water and sanitation, which has directly reduced the spread of infectious disease.

Still, this phenomenon has a side that is hard to underestimate: it exerts mounting pressure on public health spending and dramatically reshapes the outlook for pension systems, labor markets, consumption patterns, and immigration policies. A seventy-year-old, on average, spends four times more on healthcare than a thirty-year-old. In the United States, for example, health expenditure has risen from about 12 percent of GDP in 1995 to roughly 18 percent today.

Within a few years—by 2030—one in six people in the world will be aged sixty or older, up from one billion in 2020 to about 1.4 billion. By 2050, that number will have doubled to over two billion, and those aged eighty and above will have tripled to 426 million.[1]

[1] World Health Organization, "Ageing and health" fact sheet, October 1, 2025. Available at: https://www.who.int/news-room/fact-sheets/detail/ageing-and-health (Accessed October 27, 2025).

The picture is further complicated by the growing share of the world's population living in urban areas—a trend that shows no sign of reversing. Meanwhile, the global population as a whole continues to grow, having surpassed 8.2 billion. China now ranks second with 1.408 billion inhabitants, having recently been surpassed by India, with 1.420 billion. They are followed by the United States (344 million), Indonesia (285 million), Pakistan (255 million), and Brazil (212 million).

Population aging, particularly in developed countries, may be one of the pivotal forces reshaping the world before our eyes. While global population has grown, fertility rates have been declining since the 1970s. In countries such as Japan, South Korea, and Spain, they are now well below the replacement level, which is about 2.1 births per woman. When fertility drops below that level, the population begins to shrink, affecting the global demographic balance and the ratio between workers and retirees: more and longer-lived dependents supported by a smaller, less stable workforce. In developed economies across Europe and North America—where demographic growth is stagnant or declining—the aging population will translate into higher health and pension costs. By contrast, in countries such as India, population growth may offer a demographic advantage in terms of labor supply. Are we witnessing the first tectonic shifts of a new global map?

Life expectancy strongly correlates with health spending. In high-spending countries—such as the United States, Switzerland, Norway, Iceland, Canada, and Australia—life expectancy ranges between 78 and 84 years. Robust health systems and high GDP shares devoted to care reflect a mix of factors: aging populations, efficiency in service delivery, and saturation in medical expenditure. In developing nations, especially in Africa and Asia, the dynamics differ: rising health spending reflects population growth, chronic diseases, and the urgent need for infrastructure. Meanwhile, low-income countries tend to experience the fastest demographic expansion. Africa, in this global landscape, stands out as the region with the greatest demographic potential. If these nations play their cards wisely, they could unlock a horizon of significant economic expansion. Yet demographic growth alone does not guarantee prosperity. Burkina Faso and Senegal are paradigmatic examples—situated at the intersection of low per-capita GDP and high growth in the working-age population.

The outlook is complex and pressing: health and illness—or, in existential terms, the cycle of life and death—may well prove to be the Gordian knot of the world now taking shape.

Investment Case Study: Fortis Healthcare (FORH IN)

Our investment style includes investing in businesses that grow, have great management teams, high return on invested capital and good corporate governance. We initiate investments in these companies when we identify a good entry point.

Fortis Healthcare is one of the largest private hospital chains in India, headquartered in Gurgaon and operating a network that includes both high-complexity and specialized care centers as well as diagnostic facilities. Its integrated model allows the company to cover the entire health-care value chain by combining scale, quality, and operational efficiency.

Our investment in the company exemplifies our investment philosophy: to buy businesses with strong growth prospects for the 6coming years and, crucially, to begin building a position when we identify a favorable entry point. Many of the emerging markets in which we invest grow at rates far exceeding those of developed economies; consequently, companies in these markets also expand faster than their developed-market counterparts. India's real GDP has grown on average by about 6 percent per year over the past decade, and we believe it will continue to grow at similar rates in the short and medium term.

The country's per-capita GDP currently stands at approximately USD 2,600 and is heading toward the 10,000-dollar threshold within the next two decades. The comparison with China is almost inevitable. Both nations are home to populations of roughly 1.4 billion people, and twenty years ago China's per-capita GDP was also around 2,000 dollars. When it joined the World Trade Organization, Beijing began reforming its economy toward a more market-oriented and globally integrated model; today, its per-capita GDP is approximately USD 12,600. In a similar fashion, India has undertaken structural reforms in recent years. It is worth noting that other emerging economies—Vietnam, Indonesia, Bangladesh, China, and Ethiopia among them—share relatively low per-capita GDP levels and similar growth dynamics.

In addition to India's macroeconomic momentum, the healthcare industry itself offers compelling growth prospects thanks to the country's demographic dividend. The share of adults and elderly people within the global population is rising, and this group consumes more health-related products and services than any other age group. In countries such as India, where the population remains young, the expansion of the healthcare sector is likely to be even stronger. India currently has about 1.3 hospital beds per 1,000 inhabitants, compared with 7.8 in Germany and 12.5 in Japan. As the country develops and its population ages, the ratio of hospital beds per capita will gradually approach that of advanced economies.

For companies such as Fortis—whose valuation multiples on EBITDA and earnings are high—it is crucial to identify favorable entry points in order to achieve successful investment outcomes. These opportunities can arise, for instance, when a negative global headline depresses markets worldwide but has little direct impact on the company in question; when quarterly results temporarily fall below expectations; when a seemingly important piece of news about the firm turns out to be immaterial; or when macroeconomic headwinds affect performance for a particular year. During such moments, market reactions are often exaggerated, creating opportunity. We initiated our investment in Fortis Healthcare in April 2025, taking advantage of a broad decline in asset prices triggered by the United States' announcement of new tariffs on several Asian countries—a development that had little bearing on India's hospital sector.

There are several risks in failing to invest at a good entry point. First, if a stock remains flat, consolidates, or declines over a reasonable period, doubts may arise about the validity of the investment thesis. Have we overlooked something material affecting the company? Has the expected growth already been priced in? Or is heightened competition weighing more heavily than anticipated? When uncertainty grows, confidence erodes—and with it, the risk of behavioral mistakes, such as selling prematurely when the stock is merely consolidating but its long-term potential remains intact. We experienced this firsthand in 2025 with our investment in HD Hyundai Electric, initiated in early February. As the stock consolidated and drifted lower, we lost conviction and sold, only to see it resume its upward trajectory shortly thereafter.

Second, many growth companies trade at high valuations and are therefore long-term investments whose returns compound over time. Entering when prices are already elevated can lead to disappointing results even if both the company and its stock perform well.

To make sound investment decisions, it is crucial to grasp the reasons behind each stock's movements. This is learned through experience and by understanding market-behavioral biases. It fosters confidence about when to buy, add, or exit a position. Imagine playing a tennis match after having studied your opponent—knowing, for example, that he struggles with high balls to the backhand or dislikes going to the net. You would play with greater assurance and commit fewer errors. So it is with investing. We are human, and obviously mistakes are inevitable. However, great investors understand market-behavioral biases and thus minimize both the number and the magnitude of their errors.

In managing a portfolio of stocks, sizing is also crucial to maximize the return of the portfolio. We make sure we own large investments in the stocks that have the highest upside potential and for which we have high conviction that the upside will materialize. Last but not least, it is important to understand when to sell a stock. We have target prices for each of the stocks in our portfolio. However, if a stock reaches our target price, we reevaluate to understand if any of the assumptions changed. A common mistake is to be making money on an investment and to sell it early. The idea is to try to squeeze out the maximum amount of return in each of the investments.

The Technologization of Health

"*We live in a society exquisitely dependent on science and technology,*" said Carl Sagan, the extraordinary American astronomer and science communicator who brought the universe into our living rooms in the early 1980s. Healthcare is, in many ways, the field in which that maxim is now advancing at breathtaking speed.

In a world where life itself is becoming ever more valuable, the struggle to preserve it has grown both fierce and highly targeted. The giants of the healthcare industry—from pharmaceutical laboratories to hospital chains and pharmacy networks—are joining forces in strategic alliances to strengthen their position amid constant change. The reasons behind this consolidation are varied. Rising medical costs pressure industry players to optimize resources. Governments and insurance companies adjust policies and pricing. Competition intensifies and modernizes. And artificial intelligence and automation are reshaping everything from diagnosis and clinical decision-making to administrative management and medical research. Companies such as Viz. ai, whose FDA-cleared algorithms can detect strokes on medical scans and alert specialists within minutes, illustrate how AI can shorten diagnostic timelines and materially improve patient outcomes at scale.

Technology will be the physician's new stethoscope—an instrument to access the body's needs and ailments. Over the next decade, hospitals are expected to transform into *smart hospitals*: highly technologized facilities dominated by sensors, internet-connected machines, and data-monitoring systems.[2] Predictive AI will forecast patient volumes and help hospitals adjust staffing and resources; data analytics will yield sharper insight into health conditions, revealing patterns, trends, and risks that are now barely detectable; and virtual reality will assist in predicting recovery outcomes and responses to treatments or medications. By 2026, the U.S. and several European countries are facing growing physician shortages, prompting health-care systems to expand the use of AI-driven triage and diagnostic support tools to improve efficiency and help clinicians focus on more complex cases.

In advanced cardiac centers, surgeons can create patient-specific 3D digital models from imaging data to plan complex procedures and better understand anatomical fit.

Prevention, in an era of demographic swings and aging populations, could become a genuine priority. This will demand closer collaboration and integration among hospitals, outpatient centers, insurers, and other sector participants.

Cancer causes close to 10 million deaths annually worldwide, and late-stage diagnosis significantly increases mortality and treatment costs. Liquid biopsy technologies are emerging as a promising tool for earlier detection through blood-based testing, with multi-cancer screening assays currently under clinical evaluation. By 2026, AI diagnostic algorithms can process medical images

[2] Deloitte Insights, "2025 Global Health Care Outlook: Survey highlights health-system leaders' plans to focus on efficiency, productivity, and patient engagement this year," Deloitte Center for Health Solutions,

at speeds far exceeding human review and, in controlled studies, have shown improved sensitivity for early-stage lung cancer compared with unaided clinicians. In practice, these systems function as decision support tools, augmenting rather than replacing physicians.

Preventive healthcare allows patients to use wearable devices to monitor their condition at home and enables physicians to detect problems early—when they are easier and cheaper to treat. It also facilitates virtual consultations, expanding access for rural populations and those with limited mobility. Much of this is already under way. But we are moving toward a future in which health insurance will not only intervene *after* surgery but will also help prevent it—or ensure successful outcomes. Instead of paying massive medical bills, insurers will shift focus to prevention, drawing on data from medical records, wearables, and lifestyle surveys to know their clients better. AI and big data will accelerate claims processing, detect fraud, and analyze health information to generate personalized recommendations and alerts. Wearable devices will become extensions of the patient, continuously tracking vital signs and transmitting them to digital systems. This *gold mine of data* will not merely determine insurance premiums—it could pave the way for truly individualized insurance plans, tailored to each person's health profile.

One sector in particular—pharmaceutical distribution—is already in the midst of profound transformation, driven by innovation and the search for greater accessibility and efficiency. Within five years, the landscape will look dramatically different. Gone will be the days of single-channel distribution. Pharmaceutical companies will partner with specialized distributors, each mastering a distinct niche: some handling temperature-sensitive cold-chain logistics, others focusing on specific therapeutic areas. Direct-to-patient delivery will become more common for certain medications, bypassing traditional intermediaries and sending prescriptions straight to those who need them.

Imagine a world where every drug is meticulously tracked, counterfeiting becomes a relic of the past, and eco-friendly packaging and distribution are the norm. Robotic automation will streamline warehouse operations and medication delivery, minimizing human error and improving logistics. Drones and autonomous vehicles will provide viable solutions for urgent or remote deliveries, especially in crises. In recent years, medical drones have been used in pilot programs to transport blood products and, in some cases, organs over challenging terrain, demonstrating the potential to reduce transport time and improve reliability where infrastructure is limited. While

January 29, 2025. Available at: https://www.deloitte.com/global/en/Industries/life-sciences-health-care/analysis/global-health-care-outlook.html (Accessed October 27, 2025).

promising, large-scale long-distance organ delivery by drone remains in early deployment. Supply chains will grow smarter through the Internet of Things and blockchain, ensuring transparency, traceability, and real-time monitoring of environmental conditions during transport and storage. Digital platforms will give all stakeholders visibility into product movement, while AI will predict demand fluctuations and supply-chain disruptions, optimizing inventory to prevent shortages or surpluses. Sustainable practices—eco-packaging, waste reduction, and optimized transportation—will further minimize environmental impact. Pharmacies will serve patients with chronic or complex illnesses, while 3D-printed drugs will enable doses and formulations tailored to individual needs. It is the era of personalization—health made to measure.

Telemedicine

Among the many changes brought by the COVID-19 pandemic—and likely here to stay—was the accelerated adoption of telemedicine. In a world facing population aging and a declining ratio of physicians per inhabitant, remote medicine promises to redefine our daily engagement with healthcare systems as the new normal. The logic is clear: as people age, mobility can become a challenge.

The telemedicine of the future will offer elderly patients medical care without the need for travel—an enormous benefit.

Telemedicine is more accessible, efficient, cost-effective, and flexible than the traditional office visit. Patients in remote or underserved areas can receive care without leaving home. Waiting times shrink, scheduling options expand, and diagnoses arrive faster—at lower cost for both providers and patients. Those with chronic illnesses can be monitored and treated remotely, while specialists can participate in cases from anywhere in the world. With the expansion of 5G and advanced connectivity, remote robotic surgery has advanced in controlled settings, enabling specialist support across distance. However, long-distance transcontinental procedures remain technically complex and are not yet standard clinical practice.

Many older adults already use wearable devices to track vital signs or activity levels. Telemedicine platforms can integrate these data, giving physicians real-time access to crucial patient information. Forgetfulness, a common issue among seniors, can lead to missed or duplicated doses; digital platforms can send reminders and allow providers to oversee medication adherence. Although online transmission and storage of medical data raise legitimate security and privacy concerns—and not every condition can be diagnosed without physical examination—the market is set to expand rapidly. According to Fortune Business Insights, the global telemedicine market was valued at USD 104.64 billion in 2024, projected at USD 111.99 billion for 2025, and expected to reach USD 334.8 billion by 2032.[3]

Health professionals must therefore be trained in telemedicine practices, and patients educated to use these platforms effectively. Governments and health organizations will need to adapt, developing regulations that guarantee the safety, privacy, and efficacy of remote care. There is little doubt that telemedicine has the potential to revolutionize global healthcare—particularly in emerging markets.

Mobile Health

A natural spin-off of this story is that, as lifestyle-related diseases become more prevalent and economic growth unlocks the vast potential of emerging markets—especially China and India—the proliferation of wearable devices for remote health monitoring will reach an unprecedented scale.

Remote monitoring allows continuous follow-up of patients in their own homes through mobile medical devices that collect data such as temperature, blood pressure, or glucose levels. What is now known as *mobile health* (mHealth)—healthcare and medical information supported by mobile devices—will soon take a quantum leap. Increasingly, people will carry or even have implanted medical devices within their bodies, a market expected to reach USD 800 billion by 2030.[4]

Beyond the now-common smartwatch tracking heart rate, new devices will act as blood-pressure monitors or biosensors measuring oxygen, glucose, sleep quality, body temperature, pulmonary conditions, and postoperative recovery. The benefits are striking: remote, real-time access to vital health

[3] Fortune Business Insights, "Telemedicine Market: Size, Share & Growth Analysis, By Type, By Application, By Modality, By End-User, And Regional Forecast, 2024–2032" (Report ID 101067). Available at: https://www.fortunebusinessinsights.com/industry-reports/telemedicine-market-101067 (Accessed October 27, 2025).

[4] KPMG LLP, "Medical devices 2030: Making a power play to avoid the commodity trap," 2018. Available at: https://kpmg.com/us/en/articles/2023/medical-devices-2030 (Accessed October 27, 2025).

data—a matter of life and death for low-income or rural populations lacking medical services—better medication adherence through alerts and reminders, and greater efficiency for medical staff. The Association of American Medical Colleges warns that the United States alone could face a shortage of up to 86,000 physicians by 2036. Portable medical devices will fill part of that gap by transmitting patients' physiological data remotely, freeing hospital beds and allowing physicians to monitor vital signs regardless of location. Early detection of problems—before they become severe—will improve outcomes and, ultimately, safeguard what matters most: our health.

Redrawing the Genetic Map

In January 2022, the first genetically modified pig heart was transplanted into a human being. To achieve this, the donor pig underwent a series of alterations: four genes were inactivated, including three associated with strong immune rejection and one involved in growth, to prevent the heart from continuing to expand after transplantation. Six human genes were also inserted to make the porcine organ more compatible with the human immune system. This is not science fiction but gene therapy—a field that feels as though it belongs to science fiction—and it is already bringing about a Copernican revolution in medicine by creating previously unimaginable treatment possibilities and approaching the cure of diseases once deemed incurable.

If we were to zoom into our cells, we would find thousands of genes providing the instructions for producing the specific proteins and enzymes that make up the human body. A gene can be defective or missing from birth, or it can change or mutate over time, altering protein production and causing illness. Until recently, medicine focused on supplementing the proteins the body could not produce properly. Gene therapy, by contrast, goes to the root of the problem: replacing or modifying faulty genes themselves. It alters or removes genetic material within a person's cells to treat or prevent disease. In December 2017, for example, the U.S. Food and Drug Administration approved a gene therapy called Luxturna to treat a rare hereditary form of blindness. Luxturna uses a naturally occurring adeno-associated virus, genetically engineered through recombinant-DNA techniques, to deliver a healthy copy of the human RPE65 gene to retinal cells so that they can again produce the protein that converts light into electrical signals—restoring vision.

Gene editing is mainly achieved using specialized proteins that can be programmed to target specific strands of DNA within a cell. DNA strands—the building blocks of life—carry the genetic information essential to all organisms. There are several editing methods: the "pencil," the "scissors," and even a kind of "search-and-replace" processor for DNA. The best known is the CRISPR system, which acts like molecular scissors, making precise cuts that allow the deletion or replacement of particular genes.[5] Similar techniques, such as TALEN and ZFN, are taking us rapidly toward the realm of genomic medicine, where DNA is not merely a code to decipher but a fabric to edit, modify, and enhance.

Gene editing has potential applications across a wide range of highly significant medical conditions, such as hemophilia, Tay–Sachs disease, cystic fibrosis, and Huntington's disease—all caused by mutations in a single gene, or *monogenic disorders*. Before the development of these techniques, medicine had only limited capacity to treat them. Therapeutic options traditionally focused on managing symptoms and complications associated with these disorders rather than addressing their underlying genetic causes. For instance, the treatment of viral infections typically relied on drugs that inhibited viral replication or killed the virus itself. CRISPR technology, by contrast, can directly eliminate or deactivate viral genes. Similarly, the I-CreI endonuclease is a gene-editing tool that can be used to remove HBV DNA from the liver, potentially leading to a cure for chronic hepatitis B and preventing the development of hepatocellular carcinoma.

Roughly 80% of rare diseases have a genetic origin, yet most are treated today with lifelong, high-cost therapies. CRISPR-based gene editing introduces a radically different logic: one-time interventions that can replace chronic treatments costing USD 200,000–500,000 per patient per year.

This transformative capacity could revolutionize medicine—curing genetic disorders, combating chronic disease, and even expanding human capabilities. Unsurprisingly, it defines one of the fastest-growing markets: expected to rise from USD 9.78 billion in 2024 to USD 25 billion by 2030.[6] As with every historic scientific leap, however, it brings ethical, social, and economic questions that are only beginning to emerge on the horizon.

[5] U.S. Food and Drug Administration, "What Is Gene Therapy? How Does It Work?" Consumer Updates. Available at: https://www.fda.gov/consumers/consumer-updates/what-gene-therapy-how-does-it-work (Accessed October 27, 2025).

[6] Grand View Research, "Genome Editing Market Size & Share | Industry Report, 2030." Available at: https://www.grandviewresearch.com/industry-analysis/genome-editing-market (Accessed October 27, 2025).

From Chemistry to Biology

The pharmaceutical industry is also undergoing its own transformation as small-molecule (chemical) drugs give way to biologicals. For the past century, simple chemical structures have dominated medicine—from the antibiotics that revolutionized infection control to the antiretrovirals that turned HIV into a manageable chronic condition.

The use of chemicals to cure and prevent disease goes back thousands of years. Ancient Egyptians, Greeks, and Romans used natural compounds such as opium, quinine, and belladonna to relieve pain and treat various ailments. In the Middle Ages, new chemicals such as mercury and arsenic were introduced—often toxic, but precursors to modern pharmacology. The twentieth century brought a revolution: organic chemistry enabled the synthesis of safer, more effective drugs. Aspirin, first synthesized in 1897, became one of the world's most popular remedies for pain and inflammation.

Alexander Fleming's discovery of penicillin in 1928 was a decisive moment, transforming medicine by making once-lethal infections curable. The following decades saw the development of synthetic antibiotics, antidepressants, antipsychotics, and antivirals—all revolutionizing healthcare and saving millions of lives.

Today, most prescription and over-the-counter drugs are chemically based. Vaccines contain chemical adjuvants that help the body develop immunity. Chemicals are also essential in medical devices such as implants, stents, and catheters and in diagnostic tests ranging from blood and urine analyses to imaging. The global pharmaceutical market—driven largely by these traditional drugs—is projected to reach USD 1.6 trillion by 2028.[7] Their advantages are clear: they are easy to synthesize, inexpensive, predictable, and orally administered. Yet their era of dominance is ending. The age of biological medicines has begun. These complex drugs—produced through living systems or molecular engineering—offer more effective treatments with fewer side effects. They target conditions that once had no cure or could only be managed symptomatically, including cancers, autoimmune diseases, and hereditary disorders.

Biotechnology is a rapidly expanding field: in 2022 it reached USD 1.37 trillion and could hit USD 3.9 trillion by 2030. Biopharmaceuticals account for most innovative medicines and could reach USD 700 billion by 2030,

[7] Evaluate Pharma, "Evaluate forecasts global pharmaceutical market to be worth US$1.6 trillion in 2028," press release. Available at: https://www.evaluate.com/press_release/evaluate-forecasts-global-pharmaceutical-market-to-be-worth-1-6tn-in-2028/ (Accessed October 27, 2025).

roughly triple the growth of traditional pharmaceuticals. These therapies include proteins (such as monoclonal antibodies), nucleic acids (DNA and RNA), and living microorganisms like viruses or bacteria. Notable examples include monoclonal antibodies for cancer and autoimmune diseases, mRNA vaccines for COVID-19 (Pfizer-BioNTech and Moderna), and cell therapies involving transplantation of entire cells—such as stem cells to regenerate tissue damaged by chemotherapy or Parkinson's disease. Tissue engineering and regenerative medicine aim to repair or replace the function of organs affected by age or disease. Bio-artificial organs—lab-grown skin or bladders—are already being tested.

Bioinformatics, an interdisciplinary field using computational methods to analyze biological data, further accelerates discovery. Genome sequencing helps identify disease-associated genes; drug-discovery algorithms predict molecular interactions with biological systems. Machine-learning models now enable highly accurate predictive simulations, cutting costs and reducing unnecessary experiments.

As *The Lancet* noted in its August 2023 article "Artificial Intelligence in Medicine: For a Safe and Equitable Future," the meteoric rise of generative AI offers extraordinary potential but also demands caution. "How," the journal asked, "can the medical community navigate the challenges posed by artificial intelligence to harness its benefits for health?" The answer, once again, lies in balance: *we are still in time to create the future we want.*

Eat, Live, Do Not Fall Ill

Throughout history, when we spoke of health, we usually meant its absence—that is, disease. But the health of the future will increasingly mean the pursuit of *well-being*. As noted earlier, prevention will be the heart of medicine in the years ahead, and prevention begins with what we do with our bodies—and what we eat.

Over the past fifty years, the global map of disease and death has shifted dramatically. In 1969, infectious diseases and poverty-related conditions—from malaria and tuberculosis to acute respiratory infections—were the world's leading causes of death. Since then, demographic changes, medical advances, and greater awareness of health have transformed the picture. By 2023, as the planet emerged from a pandemic that exposed vulnerabilities in health systems worldwide, vaccines and treatments had sharply reduced infectious-disease mortality, while chronic noncommunicable diseases such as diabetes, cancer, and heart disease became dominant, causing more than

41 million deaths annually. Overweight and obesity will affect more than half of the global population by 2035.

It is no surprise, then, that options for sustainable nutrition—alternative proteins, cultured meat, carbon-footprint labeling, and plant-based diets—are transforming food technology and the booming wellness industry, which is growing by 5–10 percent annually.[8] This marks the rise of a powerful trend accompanying biomedicine: personalized nutrition—the use of genetic information, biomarkers, gut microbiota, lifestyle factors, and health conditions to design functional foods with benefits beyond basic nutrition. These include probiotics, prebiotics, antioxidants, plant sterols, natural anti-inflammatories, vitamins, nutraceuticals, Omega-3s, and other bioactive compounds. In essence, it is a futuristic, personalized version of the old first-aid kit—one that takes to the extreme the timeless maxim of Hippocrates: "Let food be thy medicine and medicine be thy food."

[8] McKinsey & Company, "Wellness in 2030," July 22, 2021. Available at: https://www.mckinsey.com/industries/consumer-packaged-goods/our-insights/wellness-in-2030 (Accessed October 27, 2025).

9

The New Consumer

The most common question in business is why. It's a good question, but another equally valid one is why not?

Jeff Bezos

Have we always been consumers? Or is consumption something we gradually developed and expanded throughout the twentieth century—an additional layer that came to define our identity as citizens? In truth, the idea of human beings as *consumers* began to take shape before the First World War and spread widely across the United States during the 1920s. The expansion of capitalism in the twentieth and twenty-first centuries lifted hundreds of millions of people out of poverty while generating a consumption model that gave rise to an entirely new social and economic phenomenon. As the German philosopher Herbert Marcuse observed, "people recognize themselves in their commodities."

Historically, thrift and saving were the dominant habits of most of humanity, reflecting a lifestyle in which spending beyond essentials—food, clothing, shelter—was out of reach. Yet toward the end of the eighteenth century, with the advance of industrialization in Britain, the first real process of mass production (and therefore of mass consumption) began. Even in diet, the average person gained access to greater variety: a step beyond mere subsistence. But this improvement in food diversity did not immediately extend to durable goods. The proliferation of shops and department stores served mainly a small, urban middle class in Europe. Still, the public display of desirable goods expanded dramatically and became a key driver of fashion across all social groups.

P. M. Danziger, *Capital (R)evolution*,
https://doi.org/10.1007/978-3-032-31602-8_9

The period following the Second World War marked the true beginning of mass consumption across the industrialized world, but its roots had already begun to grow around the turn of the century.

In the United States, retail stores expanded rapidly during the 1890s, mail-order catalogues appeared, and the new century saw multistory department stores covering entire city blocks. Retail was shifting from small shops to large emporia that benefited from investment capital and mass production powered by fossil fuels. By 1920, U.S. output was more than twelve times higher than in 1860, while the population had merely tripled.

As the Australian historian Kerryn Higgs notes in *Collision Course: Endless Growth on a Finite Planet*, electrification proved crucial to the spread of new types of durable goods. The percentage of U.S. households connected to electricity doubled between 1921 and 1929—from 35 to 68 percent. This was followed by a rapid proliferation of radios, vacuum cleaners, and refrigerators.

Desire began to replace need as the motor of consumption. Progress itself came to mean the continual substitution of old wants with new ones, of one product by another. In a 1929 article titled *"Keep the Consumer Dissatisfied,"* Charles Kettering, then head of General Motors Research Laboratories, wrote: "It's a matter of change—change all the time—and it will always be so, because the world moves in only one direction: the direction of progress."

Neither the 1929 Crash nor the Second World War ended this process. It is true that nearly two decades passed before mass consumption regained its central role in economic life, but once the war ended, the culture of consumption took off again throughout the industrialized world—driven by the rise of the middle class and a revolutionary new medium: television. The stage was set for the democratization of consumption on a scale previously unimaginable.

The Emerging Consumer

The world we inhabit today may seem far removed from that of the twentieth century, yet it was in that earlier era that the rise of the middle classes first took shape—a phenomenon still key to understanding today's shifting patterns of global consumption. What has changed most dramatically is geography. For companies seeking new frontiers of growth and expansion, opportunity now lies not only in the industrialized world but, above all, across emerging markets such as India, China, Indonesia, Pakistan, Bangladesh, the Philippines, Egypt, Vietnam, Brazil, and Mexico. In these countries, the past two decades have witnessed a remarkable surge in middle-class households whose economic ascent is transforming both local and global demand.

The logic is simple: as people's incomes rise, their needs and desires evolve in tandem. New possibilities redefine how they live, dress, travel, eat, and care for their health. Yet the world of commerce—whose DNA has always been change—is now being reshaped by technological innovation. In this transformation, the new and increasingly affluent middle class of emerging nations will play a decisive role in defining the future of the global economy.

Consider India, now the world's fourth-largest economy and the most populous country in the world, with more than 1.4 billion people, having recently surpassed China. India's middle class is projected to reach 715 million people by 2030, up from 432 million in 2020—an extraordinary and promising expansion by any measure. China, of course, has already walked much of this path. Its middle class has been the driving force of national—and to a large extent global—economic growth over recent decades. Although that explosive pace has slowed, the share of China's population belonging to the middle class is set to rise from about 10 percent in 2009 to over 70 percent by 2030. This evolution has produced—and will continue to produce—seismic shifts in consumption patterns, lifestyles, and economic policy, with consequences that reverberate worldwide. Closely linked to this phenomenon is another transformation shaping our century: the urbanization of the planet. The steady migration from rural areas to cities has created vast new employment opportunities and a corresponding rise in income, generating unprecedented demand—for both goods and services—in terms of both scale and variety. One additional variable must be emphasized: youth. The world's younger generations are growing in number, and their preferences are driving a profound transformation that goes far beyond demographics.

Among the trends with the greatest momentum—propelled by these young consumers—is e-commerce. In the seemingly infinite digital universe, cutting-edge electronic devices are not only coveted products in their own right; they also open doors to new possibilities, elevating the consumer experience to unprecedented levels of personalization and satisfaction.

Across emerging markets, the variety of successful e-commerce businesses is astonishing. From VIPShop in China, which sells branded clothing at accessible prices through an outlet model, to Zomato in India, a pioneer in food delivery and "quick commerce"; from Gojek and Telkom Indonesia in Southeast Asia to Voyager Innovations in the Philippines; from OXXO in Mexico to MRV in Brazil—the retail trends of emerging economies reveal a remarkable dynamism and precision in adapting to the needs and preferences of a new generation of consumers. These consumers embody what could be called the *glocal* spirit taken to its ultimate expression: for the first time, globalizing trends and hyper-personalized expectations converge within the same individual. As Ruth Crowley, vice president of customer experience design at Lowe's, succinctly put it, *"Customer experience is not an initiative. It's a mindset."* By 2026, "Quick Commerce" has expanded into electronics, with platforms like Blinkit (formerly Zomato) in cities such as Mumbai now delivering smartphones within minutes.

Looking at the present—and the decade ahead—the winning formats, in my view, are convenience stores, cash-and-carry outlets, and e-commerce platforms. The ones steadily losing market share are traditional supermarkets and hypermarkets.

Convenience Stores: The World in Your Hand

Cities grow denser and more complex. Minutes vanish faster than ever, yet time itself feels more valuable than before. People demand solutions that are not only faster but also more personal. The centrifugal forces of modern life pull us in opposing directions, creating the constant tension we feel most acutely in our daily routines. It is here that commerce acquires an almost existential character: how do we reconcile our everyday needs except by simplifying access to everything that allows us to carry on with our lives? In this landscape, convenience stores—the undisputed queens of urban Asia—emerge as oases amid the desert of modern cities.

Their advantages are self-evident. To begin with, they offer immediate access to essential items—from cold drinks and hot meals to medicines and electronic accessories—without the need to wander through endless aisles or get lost among overcrowded shelves. But the secret of their success goes far beyond that. Convenience stores are, by definition, the natural habitat of busy lifestyles, offering a coveted combination: the satisfaction of our most urgent, time-pressed needs and the comforting warmth of a small neighborhood shop, open all day—and almost all night. Strategically located, they have become urban landmarks for office workers, young people, and travelers alike. Here, one can grab a takeaway coffee or blend a fresh smoothie to taste, withdraw cash, find a last-minute gift, or stock up on quality liquor before heading to a friend's house. Speed, practicality, variety, quality—whoever coined the term "convenience store" was not being rhetorical.

Technology has accelerated this evolution. The introduction of self-checkout counters, mobile ordering, and contactless payment systems is transforming the customer experience. We are still living in the physical phase of retail, but the fusion between stores and digital technology is already underway. *"We're in the uncanny valley of retail,"* explains Brian Gill, vice president of technology at Nordstrom. *"Technology has advanced to the point where it sometimes interferes with the customer experience. But soon it will move beyond that—stepping back and letting the experience shine."*[1]

Driven by shifting consumer preferences and demographic change, the convenience-store industry is undergoing a structural transformation. The global market is expected to grow at an annual rate of 5.6 percent, surpassing US $3 trillion by 2030,[2] led by Southeast Asia and Africa. In emerging markets such as India and China, expansion will depend on accessibility—digitalization and mobile payments will play a crucial role—while in developed markets like the United States and Europe, competition will focus on innovation and differentiation, with niche formats tailored to specific lifestyles.

In short, the convenience-store industry is poised to lead a major transformation of global retail, combining innovation, sustainability, and adaptability.

The defining players of this race are the "big three": 7-Eleven, Circle K, and FamilyMart. In emerging markets, their most dynamic challengers include Freshippo, OXXO, Ipiranga, and OK Market.

7-Eleven, the world's largest convenience-store chain, operates more than 85,000 locations in some twenty countries. Its success lies in capitalizing on the demand for quick purchases through strategic locations, a broad assortment of products, and 24-hour service that perfectly matches the rhythms of urban life. Circle K operates more than 14,000 stores in forty countries, with its strongest presence in North America. Its key advantages are product variety, competitive pricing, and a brand-driven loyalty program, backed by the scale of its Canadian parent Alimentation Couche-Tard, which acquired the chain in 2003. FamilyMart, meanwhile, dominates Asia with over 28,000 stores, primarily in Japan, Southeast Asia, and Taiwan. Its emphasis on private-label

---

[1] Encyclopaedia Britannica, *"Uncanny Valley,"* https://www.britannica.com/topic/uncanny-valley (Accessed October 26, 2025). "Theoretical relationship between the human likeness of an object and the viewer's emotional response to it. The hypothesis originated in a 1970 essay by Japanese roboticist Masahiro Mori, who proposed that as a robot's appearance becomes more humanlike, our affinity for it increases—until it approaches near-perfect resemblance. At that point, the sense of familiarity abruptly gives way to unease or revulsion. Affinity rises again only when the likeness becomes fully human. This sharp dip in emotional response creates a 'valley' in the curve of familiarity."

[2] SkyQuest Technology Consulting. "Global Convenience Stores Market Size, Share, Growth, and Forecast, 2024–2031." https://www.skyquestt.com/report/convenience-stores-market (Accessed October 26, 2025).

products and partnerships with local brands has been central to its success, though its expansion outside Asia has been more limited.

In China, where the middle class has redefined consumption itself, the quintessential example is Freshippo (also known as *Hema*), part of the Alibaba Group. It integrates online and offline shopping, offering a tech-driven experience aligned with the country's e-commerce revolution. In Latin America, the Mexican giant OXXO has pioneered customer-service and self-payment technologies. In Brazil, Ipiranga operates more than 6,000 stores at gas stations under the *am/pm* brand, while Chile's Cencosud runs over 600 outlets under the *OK Market* brand.

Yet technology is not the only star of the convenience revolution. As health and wellness play a greater role in consumer choices, these stores increasingly offer fresh and healthy products, sustainable packaging, and responsibly sourced goods. The reduction of plastic, energy-efficient operations, and eco-friendly supply chains are becoming essential features to attract consumers concerned with both personal and planetary well-being.

The new ten commandments of success for convenience stores will include improving accessibility and expanding reach, competing on equal footing with restaurants and supermarkets, building strong customer loyalty programs, forming partnerships with other retail formats such as cafés and service stations, and responding almost instantly to emerging consumption trends.

Cash & Carry: Retail's Noah's Ark

In this vast and ever-expanding retail universe, midway between traditional retail and large-scale wholesale, lies the cash-and-carry model—a format that appeals most strongly to small merchants, entrepreneurs, and families seeking bulk products at competitive prices. The story began in 1954, when Sol Price created *FedMart*, the first warehouse-style store in San Diego, California. Their concept defied the conventional supermarket model by offering high-quality products at significantly lower prices through wholesale purchasing and operational efficiency.[3] Two decades later, the Price family launched a revolution in retail with the birth of Price Club—a quantum leap that transformed grocery shopping by limiting product selection to a carefully curated

[3] "I Mean Business: Sol Price and the FedMart Story," San Diego Reader, April 1, 1982. https://www.sandiegoreader.com/news/1982/apr/01/cover-mean-business-sol-price-and-the-fedmart-sto/ (Accessed October 26, 2025).

range of premium brands. Price Club negotiated lower prices with suppliers and passed those savings directly to its members, attracting a loyal customer base drawn by its no-frills design and unbeatable deals. Its popularity soared, enabling rapid expansion across the United States until it became a household name and the archetype of bulk shopping. It is hardly surprising that Price Club eventually merged with Costco, another iconic American brand that carried forward the warehouse-club model. The Prices did not retire. Instead, they founded PriceSmart, a membership-based warehouse-club chain that has operated across Latin America and the Caribbean since 1996, when it opened its first store outside the United States in Panama City.

Since then, the success of the cash-and-carry model has rested on a clear focus: product selectivity and scale. By concentrating on a limited number of brands per category, these stores carry smaller inventories than traditional supermarkets and use their concentrated volume to negotiate better terms with suppliers. They buy in bulk, obtain lower unit costs, and sell at lower prices. The result is a simplified operation that minimizes storage, inventory management, and labor costs.

The warehouse-club and cash-and-carry market is projected to grow from around US $667 billion in 2025 to nearly US $1 trillion by 2033.[4] Around 10 percent of today's global revenue is generated by the segment's star performer, Costco—which defines itself, without ambiguity, as "a large warehouse that sells goods in bulk at low prices to cash-paying customers who carry their purchases out themselves." Founded in 1983, Costco has become the world's largest warehouse-club network, with roughly 900 stores in fourteen countries, offering everything from groceries and electronics to furniture in wholesale quantities at competitive prices. Costco consistently maintains membership renewal rates above 90 percent, reflecting strong customer loyalty. Its limited assortment model, offering roughly 4,000 carefully selected items compared with tens of thousands in traditional supermarkets, reinforces a perception of curated value and trust in an era of overwhelming consumer choice. Following close behind Costco is Schwarz Gruppe, the German retail conglomerate that owns several cash-and-carry and discount chains, including Lidl—with over 11,000 stores in thirty-two countries—and Kaufland, with approximately 1,400 hypermarkets in eight nations. In a sense, this model combines the best of both worlds: connecting global supply chains with the

[4] Proficient Market Insights. *"Warehouse Clubs Market – Global Forecast to 2033."* July 10, 2025. https://www.proficientmarketinsights.com/market-reports/warehouse-clubs-market-2873 (Accessed October 27, 2025).

new patterns of consumption that are transforming economic, productive, and social systems worldwide.

Investment Case Study: Mercado Libre (MELI) and Sea (SE)

It is key to identify the best management teams.

In every instance where we have succeeded in multiplying an investment several times over the long term, four key factors have always been present:

1. The capability and quality of management.
2. The existence of genuine growth potential.
3. The existence of sustainable competitive advantages that allow the company to maintain a high return on invested capital (Porter's analysis)
4. Strong corporate governance, ensuring that minority shareholders are aligned with controlling shareholders and the decision-makers within the firm.

We began investing in Mercado Libre in 2011. Even then—when few believed it—we recognized that it had the potential to meet all four criteria. Mercado Libre is now the largest e-commerce company in Latin America.

Understanding the management team behind a company is critical; it provides confidence in times of uncertainty. This is one of the reasons our investment professionals are drawn from the same regions where we invest. In emerging markets, in particular, knowing the local culture and people makes it far easier to discern which companies truly have top-tier leadership. To gauge this, I often ask graduates from leading universities where they most aspire to work. Emerging markets are heterogeneous—culturally, structurally, and politically—and only those who live and breathe these realities can perceive the nuances that make all the difference.

Years ago, I served on the board of the Universidad de San Andrés in Argentina. One of my fellow board members was Marcos Galperin, the founder of Mercado Libre. I used to listen carefully to everything he said, but although we met monthly, we had never spoken directly about his company. At the time, I was already managing substantial investment portfolios. One day, after a board meeting, I asked him, "When are we going to talk about Mercado Libre?"

He looked at me and said, "Where are you headed?" I replied, "Home." He smiled and said, "I'll drive you." During that short drive, he shared his vision for the company. What seemed like a casual conversation turned into the seed of one of the most successful investments of my career. Although I had already invested in Mercado Libre by that point, that meeting cemented my conviction. Over the years, I also had many conversations with Pedro Arnt, the company's then-CFO, and every time I met with their team, I came away thinking: *They're just that good.* Today, Mercado Libre has one of the strongest management teams in Latin America—if not the best.

Curiously, the company's origin story mirrors that encounter. In 1999, while Galperin was still studying at Stanford University, he often sat in the front row of Professor Jack McDonald's finance class, which was frequently attended by prominent investors. One of them was John Muse, co-founder of a major private equity firm. After class, Galperin offered to drive him to the airport. During the trip, he pitched his business idea. Muse, who rarely invested in such early ventures, was struck by his conviction. *"I'm putting my whole life and all my money into this,"* Galperin said. Impressed, Muse replied as he stepped out of the car: *"I love your idea. I want to invest in your project."*

That short exchange—spoken beside an airport ramp—became the spark that launched what is now Latin America's largest e-commerce platform. What still impresses me about Galperin is his competitiveness, discipline, and professional integrity. The day he drove me home and shared his vision, Mercado Libre was already worth billions of dollars—yet he still used that car ride to sell his idea passionately, maximizing every moment to advocate for his company. Mercado Libre competes with Amazon, both in Mexico and Brazil, and the former delivered significantly more growth in the last 10 years. Additionally, many years ago when the company started operating in Brazil, Submarino, then acquired by Lojas Americanas, was the leader by a wide margin. Mercado Libre is now the largest e-commerce company in Brazil, while Lojas Americanas entered judicial reorganization in 2023.

In 2025, we also invested in Sea Limited, the largest e-commerce firm in Southeast Asia. We believe it possesses a good management team, vast growth potential, strong competitive advantages, and good corporate governance.

E-commerce penetration in the region remains below 15 percent of total retail sales, compared to roughly 35 percent in China or the United States. The growth potential is therefore enormous—and the current pace impressive, with annual expansion near 25 percent.

Sea's fintech division also represents a major opportunity in a region marked by high informality and low banking penetration. Its advantages are clear. The company can execute same-day deliveries, supported by a logistics network that reaches nearly every corner of the countries where it operates—networks that take years to build efficiently. Many merchants who use its platform could hardly survive without it. Sea sells millions of products, and no new entrant could replicate that scale quickly—it would take years to build similar supplier relationships. Finally, its website already attracts massive traffic, another formidable barrier to entry. For all these reasons, both Mercado Libre and Sea Limited exemplify what it means to invest in companies with structural tailwinds, superior management, and enduring innovation capacity—traits that define the champions of the emerging consumer economy.

E-Commerce: I Know What I Want and I Want It Now

Sports, entertainment, reading, movies, dating, communication—every sphere of life has been transformed by the digital revolution. Could such a technological wave possibly spare something as ancient and social as commerce?

Unsurprisingly, it did not. The Internet has reshaped the very foundations of trade, beginning with e-commerce, whose share of global retail expands every year. By 2032, online sales are expected to reach around US $9 trillion,[5] accounting for more than 25 percent of worldwide retail transactions. Convenience, variety, speed, and secure payments explain its meteoric rise.

Asia leads this transformation, but its impact is universal. The top ten markets for online retail (measured by e-commerce share of total sales) are China, the United Kingdom, Indonesia, South Korea, the United States, Japan, Mexico, Singapore, Russia, and Canada.

Online shopping offers a comfort level that physical stores can hardly match: consumers can browse enormous catalogs, unrestricted by time or geography. This vastness underpins the great global platforms—Alibaba, Amazon, and Mercado Libre—yet their appeal is far from generic. They attract users seeking highly specific or niche products, allow effortless comparisons, and turn discovery itself into an act of consumption. For retailers, e-commerce often means lower operating costs than brick-and-mortar outlets, enabling discounts and sharper pricing.

The key players define the global landscape: eBay and Amazon in the United States; JD.com, Alibaba, and Pinduoduo in China; Sea Limited in Singapore; Flipkart and Meesho in India; and Mercado Libre in Latin America. Each dominates its home market.

In China's massive ecosystem, JD.com is a cornerstone—focusing on electronics and high-value appliances supported by a sophisticated logistics network that guarantees rapid delivery. Its success, however, remains primarily domestic, unlike Alibaba, which has transformed global commerce since its founding in 1999. *"My vision is to build an e-commerce ecosystem that allows consumers and companies to do business online in every possible way,"* declared Jack Ma, the company's founder and then executive chairman. Today the Alibaba Group umbrella includes Taobao, Tmall, and AliExpress, all of which have revolutionized global retail trade. Completing China's e-commerce podium is Pinduoduo, whose model centers on group purchasing and flash sales. Its ability to reach rural consumers has made it one of the country's most innovative and inclusive platforms. In China, livestream shopping represents roughly a quarter of all e-commerce sales, with top hosts capable of generating hundreds of millions of dollars in gross merchandise value during major events.

In India, the crown belongs to Flipkart. Founded in 2007 by Sachin and Binny Bansal as an online bookstore, the company evolved into a broad marketplace known for competitive pricing and constant promotions. A decade

[5] Shopify. "Global E-Commerce Statistics and Trends to Know in 2025." https://www.shopify.com/enterprise/blog/global-ecommerce-statistics (Accessed October 27, 2025).

later, it was acquired by Walmart, confirming its dominance. Another Indian success story is Meesho, launched in 2015 by Vidit Aatrey and Sanjeev Barnwal, which focuses on social commerce and empowers small businesses and entrepreneurs to build virtual shops and sell via social media.

In Latin America, Mercado Libre is synonymous with e-commerce, having expanded beyond online retail into financial services and digital advertising. In Southeast Asia, the undisputed leader is Sea Limited, founded in Singapore in 2009 and structured around three divisions: Garena (online gaming), Shopee (e-commerce), and SeaMoney (digital finance and payments).

The secret behind these companies' success lies in diversification. Each explores adjacent fields—social networks, digital marketing, and financial technology—converging to create a new phenomenon: social commerce. Platforms like Instagram, TikTok, and Facebook have ignited this revolution.

Social commerce is reshaping how we shop online—a revolution nested within another. AI-driven personalization is becoming central to retail strategy. Sea's Shopee has reported that over 70 percent of purchases come from personalized discovery channels such as recommendations, livestreams, and in-app feeds rather than traditional product searches. As noted in the chapter 6 on the Metaverse, Internet revolutions unfold like Russian dolls: each one contains another inside. In this digital sub-universe, sellers have become protagonists—whether they are global brands using livestreaming and augmented reality to attract customers, influencers monetizing their reach, or individuals discovering entrepreneurial instincts they never knew they had. Yet social commerce extends beyond promotion. It thrives on the creation of community, or at least the feeling of belonging to one—now a prerequisite for any successful digital enterprise.

Worldwide, the social-commerce market was at US$1.7 trillion in 2024 and is expected to exceed US$6 trillion by 2030, with China as its epicenter. There, social commerce is projected to surpass US $3 trillion by 2030,[6] with transactions through platforms such as WeChat and Pinduoduo alone exceeding hundreds of billions of dollars annually.

WeChat, China's dominant social-media platform, boasts more than one billion active users. It integrates chat, photo and video sharing, voice and video calls, bill payments, and online shopping—essentially combining WhatsApp, Facebook, Instagram, and PayPal into a single super-app.

[6] Global Industry Analysts. "Social Commerce – Global Market Trajectory & Analytics." June 1, 2025. https://www.marketresearch.com/Global-Industry-Analysts-v1039/Social-Commerce-41288049 (Accessed October 27, 2025).

The Future at Your Fingertips

Just as the history of commerce is inseparable from social evolution—the emergence of new social strata through economic transformation—the story of e-commerce will, in large part, be the story of millennials and Generation Z. For these generations, the Internet and online shopping are not novelties but the natural order of things. They have been the launchpad for the revolution now transforming commerce across the globe.

With nearly two billion people, millennials are the largest adult generation on the planet, representing between 21 and 24 percent of the population of every continent. Together with Generation Z, they will account for more than half of the global workforce by 2030.[7]

At the same time, emerging markets will play an equally decisive role. A large share of the next wave of Internet users will live in India, China, Brazil, Russia, and South Africa, becoming key consumers for what the next generation of digital commerce has to offer.

By that point, the world will host 9.5 billion mobile devices—more than the total human population—and average data usage will triple, rising from 15 GB to over 45 GB per month, with the sharpest increases in Southeast Asia, Latin America, and sub-Saharan Africa. This leap will be driven by 6G,[8] the sixth generation of mobile communications technology, now in development to succeed today's 5G.

If 5G represented a qualitative leap in speed and connectivity, 6G will be exponential. It will allow a high-definition movie to download in under a second, or an 8K video stream to run flawlessly—without buffering or delay. This new standard will be the perfect complement to extended reality (XR) and artificial intelligence, as well as holographic telepresence, all of which require ultra-reliable, high-capacity connections to feel natural and immersive.

According to Samsung, 6G networks will become available around 2028 and reach mass commercialization by 2030. They will also enable an emerging concept with a less technical and more poetic name: the Internet of Senses—a network of sensors capable of producing digital sensations that replicate the physical world. While phones on today's 5G networks can achieve latencies of around one millisecond, 2026 laboratory

[7] Purdue University Global. "Generational Workforce Differences: From Baby Boomers to Generation Z." https://www.purdueglobal.edu/education-partnerships/generational-workforce-differences-infographic/ (Accessed October 27, 2025).

[8] Ericsson. "6G Spectrum: Enabling the Future Mobile Life Beyond 2030." White Paper, February 2024. https://www.ericsson.com/en/reports-and-papers/white-papers/6g-spectrum-enabling-the-future-mobile-life-beyond-2030 (Accessed October 27, 2025).

tests of 6G have achieved latencies of 0.1 milliseconds. This is fast enough to transmit "haptic" data, allowing a consumer in Brazil to "feel" the texture of a silk shirt located in a warehouse in Shanghai.

What does this profound alteration of perception have to do with commerce? Much more than we might imagine. Virtual reality will allow us to buy clothes almost as if we were in a physical boutique—seeing the textures, shapes, and movement of fabrics in real time. The metaverse will enrich our experiences of concerts, films, gaming, and art, while enabling virtual stores where each purchase feels as real as imagination allows.

With the arrival of 6G, augmented and mixed reality will become part of everyday life: trying on clothes virtually, previewing furniture at home, or enjoying hybrid shopping experiences that merge physical and digital spaces. This quantum leap in how we consume goods and services is already visible in the gamification of shopping, making it ever more interactive and entertaining, and in the growing use of voice-based searches through mobile devices and virtual assistants—a U.S. market projected to reach about US$50 billion by 2030.[9]

The brightest star in this new firmament will, of course, be artificial intelligence. AI will analyze shopping behavior, preferences, and demographics to offer personalized recommendations; optimize prices dynamically in real time; and detect or prevent fraud, reinforcing both consumer trust and corporate security.

By the mid-2030s, brain-computer interfaces will allow direct communication between humans and machines, taking this integration to unprecedented levels. Meanwhile, new delivery systems using drones, robots, and autonomous vehicles will revolutionize logistics—making same-day or even instant delivery faster and more cost-effective. Payments using facial recognition, fingerprints, and other biometric identifiers will complete the loop in a self-reinforcing cycle of precision and personalization, where AI learns more about us to serve us better.

Leading e-commerce platforms adjust millions of product prices every day across their catalogs using algorithms that respond in real time to inventory levels, competitor pricing, demand patterns, and user behavior.

E-commerce will stand at the center of these innovation flows. In the coming years, all channels and technologies will converge to create a radically different retail landscape—one that is more personalized, transparent, and

[9] Grand View Research. "United States Voice Commerce Market Size, Share & Trends Analysis Report, 2024–2030." Published May 2024. https://www.grandviewresearch.com/horizon/outlook/voice-commerce-market/united-states (Accessed October 27, 2025).

sustainable. Commerce has always mirrored social change. A clear example of this new transparency is the digital product passport introduced under EU circular economy regulations, designed to provide structured data on product origin, materials, and repair or recycling pathways, with phased implementation later in the decade. In this next phase, businesses will need to keep pace with technological evolution while adopting ethical, traceable, and environmentally conscious practices throughout their supply chains. They will have to measure and reduce their ecological footprint, design packaging that minimizes waste, and ensure responsible sourcing and logistics. As Jesper Brodin, CEO of IKEA, reminds us: *It's good business to be a good business. Doing good for people and the planet will also be good for business.*

Index

P. M. Danziger, *Capital (R)evolution*,
https://doi.org/10.1007/978-3-032-31602-8

FSC
www.fsc.org
MIX
Papier | Fördert gute Waldnutzung
FSC® C083411

Kolibri 360 GmbH
Ferdinand-Jühlke-Straße 7
99095 Erfurt, Deutschland
produktsicherheit@kolibri360.de